THE JERUSALEM-HARVARD LECTURES

*Sponsored by the Hebrew University of Jerusalem
and Harvard University Press*

With thinking we may be beside ourselves in a sane sense.

Next to us the grandest laws are continually being executed.

Walden, Chapter V

A Pitch of Philosophy

Autobiographical Exercises

Stanley Cavell

HARVARD UNIVERSITY PRESS

Cambridge, Massachusetts
London, England

This book is printed on acid-free paper, and its binding materials have been chosen for strength and durability.

LIBRARY OF CONGRESS CATALOGING-IN-PUBLICATION DATA

Cavell, Stanley, 1926–
   A pitch of philosophy : autobiographical exercises / Stanley
Cavell.
   p. cm. — (Jerusalem-Harvard lectures)
   Includes bibliographical references and index.
   ISBN 0-674-66980-0 (cloth)
   ISBN 0-674-66981-9 (paper)
   1. Philosophy. 2. Philosophy, American. 3. Cavell, Stanley,
1926–. I. Title. II. Series.
B945.C273P58 1994
191—dc20
  [B]   93-47642
                                                                                CIP

∼ Contents

∿ Overture

Everyone recruited into our present academic and cultural wars seems to have an answer to the question of philosophy. Some say that philosophy is literature, some say it is science, some say it is ideology, some say it doesn't matter which of these, if any, it is. For me it matters, as it matters that each of these identifications seems contentious. Since there is no uncontested place from which to adjudicate such an issue, I take it on, in my opening chapter, autobiographically, following two guiding intuitions: first, that there is an internal connection between philosophy and autobiography, that each is a dimension of the other; second, that there are events of a life that turn its dedication toward philosophy. The second of these intuitions is expressed in the question: What is an education for philosophy? If what distinguishes the work of the philosopher is not that he or she knows anything that others do not know, then the education in question is one grounding the conviction, in words of Emerson, that "the deeper the scholar dives into his privatest, secretest presentiment, to his wonder he finds this is the most acceptable, most public, and universally true." Put otherwise, it is an education that prepares the recognition that we live lives simultaneously of absolute separateness and endless commonness, of banality and sublimity. When I accordingly characterize philosophy in terms of the claim to speak for the human—hence in terms of a certain universalizing use of the voice—I call this claim that of arrogation. And I conceive a systematic arrogation of voice, or the arrogant assumption of the right to speak for others, as the ground of the philosophizing of the later Wittgenstein and of my teacher J. L. Austin, the so-called philosophers of ordinary language.

In Chapter 2 I take up a famous encounter with Austin's work initiated by Jacques Derrida's "Signature Event Context," in which Derrida praises Austin's originality but finally reads him as succumbing to philosophy's ancient (false) emphasis on the voice, holding it, in opposition to writing, to authorize the seriousness or innerness of thought. I argue, against Derrida, that Austin and Wittgenstein, in distinguishing between metaphysical and ordinary language, distinguish between what may be called the metaphysical and the ordinary voice; but they read the harm in philosophy's bewitchment by the metaphysical voice not as the disparagement of writing (unlimited difference, strangeness, distance, and so on) but as the suffocation of the ordinary voice (my limited presentness to the world and others in it, the small differences and intimacies my existence projects), interpretable as the advent of skepticism, hence of the subjects of comedy and tragedy. And the irony of Derrida's work is that it contributes to this suffocation of the ordinary; I call it a continuation of philosophy's flight from the ordinary.

In Chapter 3 I look at the great Western institution that celebrates the human possession of, or by, voice—the institution of opera—and ask whether opera's issues can be seen to be a response to, hence a continual illumination of, the divisions of self, the suffocation of speech, and the withdrawal of the world that have preoccupied philosophy since the advent of skepticism in Descartes, which is to say, explicitly since the generation after the invention of opera and the construction of the works of Shakespeare. The material on opera builds from my past work on film (as in *The World Viewed* and *Pursuits of Happiness*) and climaxes with a discussion of Debussy's and Maeterlinck's *Pelléas et Mélisande*, still at the heart of the culture out of which Derrida speaks, and containing a striking and consequential link—forgotten or unknown—with events in American philosophy, beginning with Maeterlinck's particular devotion to the writing of Ralph Waldo Emerson.

What are here called chapters were, even before the elaborations that came with editing, considerably longer than the versions of them delivered as the Jerusalem-Harvard Lectures at Hebrew University on November 22, 24, and 26, 1992, under the title "Trades of Philosophy." No one seemed to take pleasure in that title; perhaps a reason was that the concept of trades failed to invoke the wind it names. But whatever the reason, and whatever the losses, when the idea of philosophy's pitch presented itself to me, I had to keep it. Quite apart from taking on music and baseball and vending, it speaks, not darkly, of a determined but temporary habitation and of an unsettling motion that befit the state of philosophy as a cultural fact always somewhat at odds with philosophy on its institutional guard.

A distinct consequence of preparing these texts—especially of returning to them to complete their revision, after the usual postponements called for by teaching and other obligations—has been my beginning to read Gershom Scholem and Walter Benjamin again, this time in a little more systematic way. This consequence has taken me by surprise, and I would like to recount certain passages of it by way of invitation to these pages. Almost ten years ago I read through Scholem's edition of his correspondence with Benjamin. However fascinated, I felt that for me really to delve into the intricacies and densities of central Europe in the generation of Wittgenstein and of Heidegger was hopeless without more learning at my command than I could foresee, or in the absence of an emergency that neutralizes prudence. What took me back to Scholem and his friendship with Benjamin, was, as usual, something smaller and sharper, a lingering chagrin at my inability to achieve a due density of implication in the two paragraphs in the chapters to follow— one near the end of the first, another near the end of the third—in which I seek to relate a certain progress in the Jerusalem texts, a certain surprise in their horizons, to the fact of my being in Jerusalem, or rather to my not being in Jerusalem.

In the first chapter I relate this progress to the importance, always decisive for me, of the Eastern longings, that is, the non-European longings, in the writing of Emerson and of Thoreau; that resonance in their writing should be audible in Jerusalem more practically than in any other city I had spoken in, verging East and West. Without knowing much, one could know that Scholem had devoted his life to reclaiming the mystical tradition in Judaism, a tradition to which he attributed the power to regenerate fixated religious institutions. I found myself asking what present importance Scholem attached to, or what present hope he held out for, this mystical tradition, what access he claimed to find for it in himself, what he felt he could relate it to in the modern world, which for him came under heavy judgment, politically and religiously. If the experience of this tradition was something that had had its last clear effect in the eighteenth century, in later Chasidism, what did Scholem regard as a continuation or correspondence with something current, something usable in contemporary thinking and for the contemporary spirit? Having spent much of my last decade and a half trying to show something like the present usefulness, even potential regenerativeness, of Emerson and Thoreau as thinkers, I held out some hope for myself that that pertinence, somehow, could be found to bear, however lightly, on the way that Scholem, so I recalled, thought of the Kabbalah.

I picked up a collection of Scholem's essays that I had left half read, *On Jews and Judaism in Crisis*, and began with the long interview of Scholem that opens the book. The impression of the role in which Scholem cast Kabbalah was reaffirmed in a section entitled "Into the World of Kabbalah": "I was interested in the question: Does halakhic Judaism have enough potency to survive? Is *halakhah* really possible without a mystical foundation? Does it have enough vitality of its own to survive for two thousand years without degenerating? I appreciated *halakhah* without identifying with its imperatives. The question was tied up with my dreams about the *kabbalah,* through the notion that it might be *kabbalah* that explains the survival of the consolidated force of halakhic Judaism. That was certainly one of my obvious motives." Scholem goes on to say that these questions became clear to him in the months before he went to Switzerland, where he spent the years 1917 and 1918 in Walter Benjamin's company. This statement of Scholem's confirmed my memory of his motivations, but it was not until the last page of this long interview that my instinct in returning to Scholem, and to his autobiographical reflections, was most marvelously rewarded.

He says there: "Modern man lives in a private world of his own, enclosed within himself, and modern symbolism is not objective, it is private, it does not obligate. The symbols of the kabbalists, on the other hand, did not speak only to the private individual, they displayed a symbolic dimension in the whole world. The question is whether in the reality in which today's secular person lives this dimension will be revealed again. I was strongly criticized when I dared to say that Walt Whitman's writings contain something like this. Walt Whitman revealed in an utterly naturalistic world what kabbalists and other mystics revealed in their world." That is the Emersonian connection I wanted. Why Scholem does not recognize Emerson behind Whitman, or find the link worth noting, is an interesting question, too interesting, and too pertinent to old interests of mine, for me to forgo making one guess now.

A few pages earlier Scholem had been asked about Oriental influences on Jewish mysticism. He mentions Ramakrishna and describes the book of conversations with him written down by his disciples as "an authentic document—one of the most interesting religious documents I know." He then mentions that Romain Rolland wrote a famous book about Ramakrishna. (The appearance of Rolland's name has its own interest, I suppose associated by now, vaguely, with the name of Beethoven and with the citation of him and dedications to him by Freud.) It happens that Rolland wrote a companion book about

Ramakrishna's greatest disciple, Vivekananda, who, unlike his master, visited the United States. In that book Rolland cites Whitman as the genuine, if flawed, embodiment of America's advanced spiritual state, ready to receive Vedantism, and sees Emerson as something like the facilitator and intellectualizer of this role. So Rolland continues the reception of Emerson—however discontinuous Rolland's interest is from that of Emerson's more conventional readers—in a mode of condescension. In Rolland's account, Emerson is unable to appear as a thinker with his own relation to establish between philosophy and religion, call this his own continuation of philosophy's mission in the critique of religion. It is a mission, roughly simultaneous with Marx's claim that the philosophical critique of religion is completed, that shows Marx's claim to be premature. I assume this mission provides a reasonable ground for Nietzsche's undying debt to Emerson. It also seems to me precisely pertinent to Scholem's central quarrel with Benjamin over the relation of Marx and theology. Shall we think of Scholem's passing up of Emerson as an intellectual near miss?

I do not know what Scholem was counting on in calling Whitman's world an utterly naturalistic one. Whitman tapped a stratum of nineteenth-century America that might equally be taken to characterize an utterly transcendental world, in its breathless quest for itself, its desperation to work out, to imagine, to express itself. But I am trusting Scholem's experience, even witnessing, of Whitman's writing as something that corresponds to his investments in rediscovering the receptions of Kabbalah. Hence I am putting myself in the way of a certain validation from the direction of Jerusalem, however indirect, and elsewhere perhaps unavailable, for my investment in the Emersonian event. To mark this way, I have added epigraphs to each of the three chapters to follow that are taken from Scholem's essay "Walter Benjamin and His Angel." The epigraphs sketch a story on their own, and it is not to be assumed that they are in their best positions here. For example, the epigraph to the third chapter relates a legend that Benjamin tells more than once of the creation of angels as of existences meant to sing one note of praise to God and then vanish. It may well be taken as an emblem of the ephemerality and eternality of voice, so as picturing certain dimensions of something that I say about the voice in opera, in its imitation of, or doubling of, the conditions of the voice in speech. But that epigraph could equally go in front of the first chapter because of the idea of the true name, that of the secret self, being hidden.

These epigraphs represent an entire mode of approaching aspects of matters I dwell on that is not directly or consecutively taken in my own text—aspects of voice, ephemerality, the inexcusable, name, dedication, the latency of self. Not all overtures confine themselves to the material they make way for.

But these citations mark and hold open two further ways of continuation visible from here. The most pressing for me is to continue with measures of autobiography beyond the few steps taken in these pages. I think, for example, of the end of the first epigraph, in which, when the child's Hebrew name is told him on the day of his Bar Mitzvah (thus shown to have been a secret merely empirically, not metaphysically), the father pronounces what Scholem describes as a "peculiarly sober blessing": "Praised be [He] who has removed my responsibility for this one here." Scholem's marking of the casualness, the soberness, the abruptness of this so-called blessing reminds me of an exchange with my father in his pawn shop in Sacramento, during a visit on my way from UCLA, where I had begun studying philosophy, to take up a fellowship from Harvard to continue graduate work there. Early in our exchange my father asked me whether I believed there is a God. He did not seem surprised that I was surprised and silent, and he went on. "There must be something. To deny that there is something you would have to be a fool or a genius. You've been doing nothing for three years now but studying philosophy; do you think philosophy will give you the answer to that question?" I said that from what I had so far seen of philosophy now, the question hardly seemed alive. His response was something like: "Well, now that you have this fellowship, and it looks like you might finish something you've started, I have to say that it is up to you, Rabbi, to determine." Then he told me the following story (I may have a detail or two wrong, so may he have; or he may have invented it): In the course of slaughtering a cow, a knife had broken and lodged in the cow; the question arose whether the slaughtering was to be ratified. One rabbi said that the knife was too close to a particular organ for it to have produced kosher meat. Another rabbi disagreed, arguing that the sharp edge of the knife was turned away from the organ. And my father ended: "Now it is going to be up to you, Rabbi, to decide which rabbi you agree with." Neither my father nor I believed we could participate in the casual public effectiveness of the father's blessing of autonomy cited in Scholem's story of the giving of the name at the Bar Mitzvah. So my father found an analogous form for saying to me that he, as it were, yielded to me the authority for finding my name in whatever blessings came my way.

The other way of continuation from the epigraphs takes me to the second of the paragraphs over which I expressed chagrin earlier, in their attempts to make a little explicit certain links in my lectures in Jerusalem with the fact that I am, or am not, in Jerusalem. The first (in the first chapter) invoked the non-Western longings of Emerson and Thoreau. The second (at the end of the third chapter) shows my distrust of myself either to regard Israel as one place among others (as in certain obvious respects it surely is—say, politically, morally, economically) or not so to regard it (as in its standards for itself and its memories of itself, by which it risks crushing itself, it surely is not). In the same interview in which Scholem cites Whitman and Ramakrishna, he speaks of his not believing in the formula for Israel as "like all the nations," while at the same time believing that the process of Zionism must not "[erase or blur] the borders between the religious-messianic plane and political-historical reality." One consequence for Scholem is that "Zionism was a calculated risk in that it brought about the destruction of the reality of Exile." But some American Jews must feel sometimes— some will never feel otherwise—that it is America which has destroyed that reality, that America names the place you can be a secular Jew and at home.

My father could never have said that, for all his adoration of America and, from the time I knew of such things until I left home for college, for all his idolizing of Franklin Roosevelt. His mind was forever scarred by the reports of assimilated German Jews in the decades before and between the world wars pronouncing that they were at home in Germany. I was accordingly well prepared for Scholem's contemptuousness—at the opposite extreme of Jewish culture from my father's —toward the superficiality and illusoriness of secular Jewish life in the Germany of his adolescence; and in a sense prepared for his feeling that his access to Judaism lay in Zionism, for that is where it was for my father until the formation of the state of Israel. That event took the moral heart out of him. He seemed to feel useless in the face of the actuality of Return, or doubly useless, as if incapable of contributing now to two nations. He was, so far as I know, the only member of a very large remaining family of several generations, and the only one among his closest circle of friends, who never visited Israel. Have my visits to Israel, begun late in my life, been also for him, or also against him? Hardly the only form of an old riddle.

I do not in the chapters to follow go into the issue of the ways my Jewishness and my Americanness inflect each other. I am moved to say here, however, that I can understand certain forms taken by my devotion to Thoreau and to Emerson as expressions of that issue, particularly, I suppose, my perception that they provide, in philosophizing for and against America, a philosophy of immigrancy, of the human as stranger, and so take an interest in strangeness, beginning no doubt with the strangeness of oneself. Some will see this as a clinical issue, with more bearing on myself than on those I claim to perceive. I will, I trust, be excused for seeing it also as a critical issue, enabling genuine perceptions that might otherwise go unwon.

~ 1

Philosophy and the Arrogation of Voice

In memory of Yochanan Budick

Benjamin, who published his own writings under his civil name, made no use, as he says, of this name ["Agesilaus Santander," one he had applied to himself in the short text among his literary remains that Gershom Scholem's essay undertakes to interpret]; he "proceeded . . . as did the Jews with the additional name of their children, which remains secret" and which they reveal to them only when they reach maturity. This is an allusion to the Hebrew name which every male Jewish child receives at circumcision and which is used instead of the usual civil first name in religious documents and synagogue services. In fact this name is "secret" only insofar as no use is made of it by assimilated Jews, even though their children after the completion of the thirteenth year of life—when, according to Jewish law, they reach maturity—are called up by this name for the first time in order to read from the Torah in the synagogue *(bar mitzvah)*. Among Jews this "reaching of maturity" means only that they are now obligated under their own responsibility to keep the commandments of the Torah, and that for purposes of public prayer, requiring at least ten "mature" participants, they are among those counted. Indeed, on this solemn occasion, the father pronounces a—to say the least—peculiarly sober blessing: "Praised be [He] who has removed my responsibility for this one here [*sic!*]."

Gershom Scholem, "Walter Benjamin and His Angel," pp. 216–217

The arrogance of philosophy is not one of its best kept secrets. It forever toys with worlds, and when its discoveries humble human pride, like Kant's in proving the necessary limitation of human knowledge, or Nietzsche's in interpreting our resentments, it finds itself exorbitantly superb. A formative idea in planning these lectures was to pose the question whether, or how, philosophy's arrogance is linked to its ambivalence toward the autobiographical, as if something internal to the importance of philosophy tempts it to self-importance. Arrogance and autobiography are clearly enough linked in such an outburst of Thoreau's in *Walden* as "I brag for humanity," and of Nietzsche's in *Ecce Homo* as "I have . . . given mankind the greatest gift that has ever been given it." Philosophy has equal reason to shun the autobiographical since its claim is to speak, using Kant's predicates of the a priori, with necessity and universality. Yet philosophers have left us with a trail of images of themselves preparing for philosophy or recovering from it. After the instances of Augustine's forbidden pears and Rousseau's unconfessed ribbon, we may stray from Descartes in his dressing gown sitting before the fire, or Hume's sociably returning from his closet to play backgammon, to Emerson walking across a muddy common, or Thoreau lying on the ice, looking down through a hole he has cut in it at the summer still on the floor of the pond; or to Wittgenstein resting on his spade, or Austin shooting his neighbor's donkey, perhaps by mistake, perhaps by accident.

I propose here to talk about philosophy in connection with something I call the voice, by which I mean to talk at once about the tone of philosophy and about my right to take that tone; and to conduct my talking, to some unspecified extent, anecdotally, which is more or less to say, autobiographically. To give an account of this response to the invitation to deliver the Jerusalem-Harvard Lectures—which specifies this occasion as one in which I am "to present an analysis of the problems and developments in [my] field of research and study"—may be taken as the goal of my lectures.

A practical reason for talking about myself is that in being reminded so often over the past thirty-five years how eccentric my views and ways are, I am unsure for whose views beyond mine I would be speaking. I perhaps make more of the rift between philosophical traditions than other philosophers may find productive, wishing to think, when I can, within the tear in the Western philosophical mind represented, so I believe, by the distances between the English-American and the German-French dispensations. And I perhaps harp on philosophy's differences from other perspectives more than other philosophers nowadays seem to want to do, finding it important to hold out against the idea that philosophy is science (as late positivists are still apt to assert, or assume), or that philosophy is literature (as recent French influences seem ready to allow). And when I also deny that philosophy is psychoanalysis many philosophers will want to know how I can think these fields sufficiently similar to warrant distinguishing. There are various answers to this. An ancient answer is that philosophy begins with, say, in the Socratic ambition, and may at any time encounter, an aspiration toward the therapeutic, a sense of itself as guiding the soul, or self, from self-imprisonment toward the light or the instinct of freedom. A modern answer is that I have come to distrust Freud's denial that psychoanalysis is philosophy—distrust it, you may say, on the psychoanalytic ground that Freud denies it too often. An answer more to the present purpose is the way both can deny, if rather oppositely, the pertinence to their work of the autobiographical. For philosophy, speaking for oneself is, let us say, too personal; for psychoanalysis, what we are likely to call autobiography is, in a sense, wrongly personal, about the wrong person, serving to avoid hearing (roughly paraphrasing Lacan) who it is who is dictating your history.

A somewhat more positive view of philosophy, as I see it, is given in considering its relation to its audience. Science can be said to have no audience, for no one can fully understand it who cannot engage in it; art can be said to have in each instance to create or re-create its audience. Philosophy is essentially uncertain whom in a given moment it seeks to interest. Even when it cannot want exclusiveness, it cannot tolerate common opinion. Nietzsche's *Thus Spoke Zarathustra* is subtitled *A Book for Everyone and No One;* this is comparable to Emerson's having said, with, to casual readers, casualness, that he speaks out of an "insight [that] throws us against all and sundry, against ourselves as much as others." Philosophy's essential uncertainty of its audience is what may appear as its esotericism—not its capacity to keep secrets (which I believe it precisely repudiates in its differences with religion) but its power to divide one from himself or herself, or one from others, in the name of healing or of bringing peace, so that it oscillates between seeming urgent and seeming frivolous, obscure and obvious, seductive and repellent. Thoreau in *Walden* says: "You will pardon some obscurities, for there are more secrets in my trade than in most men's, and yet not voluntarily kept, but inseparable from its very nature." I take this not as obscurantist but as open-minded, not as turning away but as turning toward, a mark of his philosophical rigor. A refrain of Nietzsche's *Ecce Homo* is "Have I been understood?"—when it is unclear that he could have been clearer. Wittgenstein is plainer: "Since everything lies open to view there is nothing to explain. For what is as it were hidden is of no interest to us." What then has philosophy to say? It is apt to be in recognition of what I call the threat of skepticism, to expose its denial of this world and of whatever its other is—often a drift in my line of philosophy.

There is a less practical reason for my turning to autobiography, and rather more systematically than philosophy's ambivalence invites: not exactly that I have become lost and am seeking to find myself (in the current state of the intellectual world, to go no further, this seems understandable enough as a cause in producing so many recent works of autobiography), but that I feel the need to recount what I have so far written, to add it up again—as if in the very achievements in which I take some pride I have kept things unsaid unnecessarily, which hence press to be said.

As for why the question of the autobiographical for me turns out to produce an opening chapter in which I think about an autobiographical dimension of philosophy, together with a philosophical dimension of the autobiographical—in terms taken from certain passages of my life that, to my ear, are crossed by ones from Thoreau's and from Nietzsche's autobiographies; and why this requires recognizing in my second chapter an encounter, or a misencounter, between Austin and Derrida that was notorious a decade and a half ago; and why in a third chapter it has seemed to me not only appropriate but irresistible to begin speculating about the existence of opera, I can at least say in my defense that these conjunctions are proposed not as containing answers to questions I regard as given but as grounds for discussions that stand no less in need of discussion than any issue they will themselves propose.

After some years of graduate study in which philosophy interested me but seemed unlikely to be moved by anything I had to say, or by the way in which I seemed fated to say it, I began finding my intellectual voice in the work of the so-called philosophers of ordinary language, J. L. Austin at Oxford and the later Wittgenstein; and, as it turns out, but took me years to recognize usefully, importantly because their philosophical methods demand a systematic engagement with the autobiographical. This should have been reasonably evident in Wittgenstein's motto: "What *we* do is lead words back from their metaphysical to their everyday use (*Philosophical Investigations*, § 116)." (This motto suggests that for Wittgenstein, while not for Austin, the title of his philosophy might equally well be the philosophy of metaphysical language. He has as fully worked out a theory of how language becomes metaphysical as he does of how language becomes ordinary, that is, of what is acquired in acquiring language.) How we "lead words back" to their everyday use may be said to be done by following Austin's apparently innocuous directive to ask ourselves what we say when (that is, in varying contexts).

Who the we is is, of course, critical, what it is the first-person plural here betokens. It does not betoken that the philosopher who practices in this way is awaiting the agreement of others; he feels, one can say, that he already has their agreement, that it is metaphysics which is the private party. The metaphysician says: We know of the feelings of others only from their behavior—but the Wittgensteinian philosopher notes that this use of "only" is suspiciously empty, it contrasts with nothing; what does the metaphysician want? Or the metaphysician says: We know things not as they are in themselves but only as they appear to us—as if this is an obvious or remarkable fact. But these ideas of a realm of appearances and of a realm of the in itself are displacements, constructions formed under forced labor, about which it is neither true nor false that we know or are aware of them. The idea of how something appears is an idea of its appearing this way rather than that way, or under these conditions rather than others. But to transfer the idea so that we speak of the senses, and so of the human body as such, as subject only and necessarily to appearances is to speak of the body as a condition under which we inhabit the world, a condition that might be otherwise. This means not that I am imagining nothing in imagining myself without a body; but that I have one is not a fact, as it is a fact that the one I have is one of such and such a size and in such and such a condition. We are not well advised to inspect the population to discover who among us in fact have bodies and who have not. Or, for one further case, the metaphysician says: Our epistemological repertory is rankable as on a divided line, with knowledge superior to belief in a certain proportion—but Austin finds that the expression "I know" does not function to introduce a claim higher in epistemological rank than "I fully believe," for there is no such higher rank; what the words do is to stake one's credibility or truthfulness or authority in a different way, rather like the difference between saying "I fully intend" and saying "I promise."

Philosophers who proceed as Austin suggests will not be much interested to poll others for their opinion about such crossroads. Then why do such philosophers say "we" instead of "I"? With what justification? They are saying what the everyday use is—of "appears," of "in itself," of "knowledge," of "promising." And by whose authority? Their basis is autobiographical, but they evidently take what they do and say to be representative or exemplary of the human condition as such. In this way they interpret philosophy's arrogance as the arrogation of the right to speak for us, to say whatever there is to say in the human resistance to the drag of metaphysics and of skepticism; and authorize that arrogation in the claim to representativeness, expressed autobiographically. There is a humility or poverty essential in this arrogation, since appealing to the ordinariness of language is obeying it—suffering its intelligibility, alms of commonness—recognizing the mastery of it.

Philosophers who shun the autobiographical must find another route to philosophical authority, to, let's say, the a priori, to speaking with necessity and universality (logic, as Kant says, is such a route), and find another interpretation of its arrogance (philosophy's inherent superiority, in intelligence or purity, is always a convenient such route).

Not to shun the autobiographical means running the risk of turning philosophically critical discourse into clinical discourse. But that has hardly been news for philosophy since its taking on of modern skepticism, since Descartes wondered whether his doubts about his existence might not class him with madmen, and Hume confessed that his thoughts were a malady for which there is no cure. If the following autobiographical experiments are philosophically pertinent, they must confront the critical with the clinical, which means distrust both as they stand, I mean distrust their opposition. (Reductive clinical discourse is as fashionable as cynicism. A good example is the inside dopester's knowledge of Thoreau's habitual, hypocritical sliding from his isolation into free, home-cooked meals, as if the official, or intended, moral of his economy were roughly Polonius's, neither to borrow nor to lend; whereas the necessity of giving and receiving, the recognition of endless indebtedness, which others imagine can be paid off, is as implicit in every word of *Walden* as its writer's mother is, in what he calls the mother tongue.)

Can it be seen that each of us is everyone and no one? Emerson famously stakes the oscillation: "I am God in nature; I am a weed by the wall" ("Circles").

Who beside myself could give me the authority to speak for us? To verify that in practice we are each in a position to give ourselves the right, take it from ourselves, as it were, was the mission of the first essay I wrote in philosophy that I still use, that is, the one in which I found my philosophical voice, or the track of it, the title essay of *Must We Mean What We Say?* It is explicitly a defense of the work of my teacher Austin against an attack that in effect dismissed that work as unscientific, denied it as a contender in the ranks of philosophy at all. (Since a response to some denial was part of my cue in taking up Thoreau and Emerson, even in thinking about Shakespeare and then about film, there is the sense of a pattern here, perhaps of further interest.) The form of the attack was to ask how philosophers of ordinary language undertook to verify their assertions about language, what they took as evidence for them, in a time when logical positivism still had no need to share institutional power and its signature charge of empirical unverifiability was the term of criticism most to be feared, and not merely in the halls of philosophy. The form of my response was to get out of the way of the charge, to construe it as largely impertinent, or too late, by attempting to demonstrate that Austin's practice was more convincing than the application to it of a philosophical theory of verification that the new practice itself should be taken to challenge.

What I was unprepared to claim, what was systematically unsaid, was that the question of verification was exactly made to miss the interest of the new work, of its new claim to philosophy's old authority, one whose power would reside in a certain systematic abdication of that authority (without resigning it to science, or to anything else). Put otherwise, I was unprepared to claim that the interest in the new philosophy lay precisely in the necessity and openness of its arrogance and autobiographicality, that these are not personal but structural features of the necessity to say what we say, that in thus laying their bodies on the philosophical line, and living to tell their tale, the likes of Wittgenstein and Austin must be tapping a dimension of philosophy as such. I was unprepared—and not just intellectually—for the intensity of hostility their work inspired, as well as for the organizational and pedagogical skills that positivism had mounted against the hostility it in its turn inspired.

Something further went unsaid in that beginning essay of mine. While I had in effect demonstrated my right to answer the methodological protocols concerning what we say when, I had not suggested the basis for my speaking for those protocols themselves, for enlisting in what Austin, in the introduction to *How to Do Things with Words*, was calling a revolution in philosophy; for, in a word, claiming my inheritance of that way of philosophy, which would mean tracing that feature of my life as a condition of my life. I mean, of course, to claim this philosophically. I have insisted that philosophy is interested in questions in its own way—call it a way in which the answer is not in the future but in the way the future is approached, or seen to be unapproachable; in which the journey to the answer, or path, or tread, or the trades for it, are the goal of it. So the life of which philosophy is a condition will be seen by philosophy to be one that can take such an interest in itself. And since I am imagining the life of philosophy to be interesting to philosophy in its commonness, its representativeness, that life will be seen in its aspect of interest to itself, or in its failure of it, in what it is that preserves its worth for itself, what payments, what deferments, allows it to go on with interest; and that is perhaps its uniqueness. The autobiographical dimension of philosophy is internal to the claim that philosophy speaks for the human, for all; that is its necessary arrogance.

The philosophical dimension of autobiography is that the human is representative, say, imitative, that each life is exemplary of all, a parable of each; that is humanity's commonness, which is internal to its endless denials of commonness.

Since I suppose I cannot know in advance which features of my life will be the telling ones here, in recounting my work, I have to tell the whole of it, up to a point. This might be done in a sentence, as in a dictionary entry, or in an entry for every day of this life, something Thoreau and Emerson nearly managed for theirs. But here, experimentally, to tell in a couple of dozen minutes my story as approaching philosophy, leaving room for a couple of dozen afterwords to respond to it, I need some clues.

The first clue is to ask why this question of autobiography is posed for me here and now, in this city and at this turn in my philosophical path. The second clue will be to ask why the question of philosophy was posed for me when and how it was, broached by the study of pragmatism and positivism for three years at UCLA, and settled, to begin with, by Austin at Harvard four years later. Pieces of this settlement with Austin will guide my second essay. Here I take up matters before and after that. No name or date of that broaching and that settlement will be more important than the fact that they occurred within the aftermath of my crisis in having left the study of music, as if philosophy occurs for me as some form of compensation for, or perhaps continuation of, the life of music. The moment is marked by my graduating from college and preparing to enter the Juilliard conservatory (for what turned out to be only a few months, mostly spent avoiding my composition lessons).

∾

Why raise these memories here, in this city? About Jerusalem—if I am not to be swamped by its relentless interrogation of my diaspora sensibility and of my sense of my father's inner ghetto—I will tell just one story, to emblematize that it is a place of stories, that each one here has a story, to begin with, the story of his or her path here, as if to make credible to oneself the sheer fact that one is here. This is surely why I feel enabled for the first time to tell in public certain fragments of mine, which is in a sense part of a story about why I am *not* here, secure in the knowledge that here it is known that you do not get to a life until you get to its pain as well as to its joys. And because here you know that the worst is known, and for that reason you know that one's specific pain, small or large, still pain, need not go unsaid and unaccompanied. No place more sternly warns that in seeking for the representativeness in your life you have to watch at the same time for your limitedness, commemorating what is beyond you. One is neither to claim uniqueness for oneself nor to deny it to others. (Perhaps this is something Emmanuel Levinas means in attributing infiniteness to the other, interpreting a passage in Descartes's Third Meditation that, on my interpretation, concerns the fate of the other in finiteness.)

The story is this. In the days before returning home at the end of my first and longest stay in Jerusalem, on and off for the first six months of 1986, the Jerusalem premiere of *Shoah* was announced at the Cinematheque. I decided against trying to get in, feeling already numb with what there was to think about, telling myself that I did not have to take this particular punishment in Jerusalem, that it could wait, and so on. A colleague I was to meet for lunch the following day phoned to say that he had forgotten when he proposed the luncheon date that it conflicted with the premiere of *Shoah*, that in view of my plans to leave I might be willing, not to miss our chance, instead of at the University to meet him at the Cinematheque in the late morning, a couple of hours before the early afternoon opening of the very long film. When we met there were almost no other people around, but after an hour or so the place began filling up and all at once, so it seemed, there were people standing in small groups talking in all the spaces between the tables throughout the restaurant. In a pause in our conversation I attended more carefully to the crowd; I realized that this event had produced the most beautifully dressed and elegantly spoken gathering of its size that I had seen in my months in Jerusalem, where a surface of studied casualness of dress and of manner otherwise, in my experience, prevailed. Moved by the timeless defiance I read in this preparation to witness yet another witnessing of the Holocaust, I turned to say something about it to my companion, who, however, spoke first: "I had decided this morning that I would not after all subject myself to this event. If you've seen the real thing in full technicolor, why look at a black and white reproduction?" So this is how it can be, I thought, to be told the common, incomprehensible fact that the person before one, also having an omelette with toast and a cup of coffee, had been in a concentration camp—including the small opening of defensive doubt that that was in fact what had been said. "But," he continued, "my wife wants to go with me—this was not part of her past—and we managed to get an extra ticket for you." Thus I learned in Jerusalem not to count very hard on plans to postpone something.

∿

Why now and why then? What in my work now calls for this autobiographical recounting, and what in my life before studies called for those trades of musical and philosophical studies?

Philosophy's native aversiveness can appear as perverseness, and I have I said that I have seemed to myself fated to take what appear as eccentric perspectives, as it were to remain between, to refuse sides. In the past few years, when I have found myself writing and publishing at a greater rate than ever before, I have been told, from both sides of the division of philosophical traditions, that I am an alternative voice. This has a friendly and a hostile face. It is the hostile that has lately come to seem to me one no longer to remain familiar with but to question. I shall, as pivot to, and I suppose as the opening moment of, the autobiographical sketch of my whole life leading to philosophy, give as an instance of something that can grate on philosophical nerves, but that I call philosophical work, an instance of what I want out of reading a familiar philosophical text.

The text is one likely to come up in anyone's reading of Wittgenstein's *Investigations* (§ 217): "If I have exhausted the justifications [for my following a rule the way I do, for speaking as I do] I have reached bedrock, and my spade is turned. Then I am inclined to say: 'This is simply what I do.'" The standing controversy about this passage turns on whether it is to be taken as Wittgenstein's confession that he has no non-skeptical solution to the possibility of the privacy of language; or whether it is perhaps an indication that a pragmatist account of "what I do" is Wittgenstein's non-skeptical explanation of our sharing of language; or—let's hope—in some further way. Consider that philosophy's distrust of, or ambivalence toward, the autobiographical, or personal, is characteristically expressed in its sense that an attention to style in writing—we might say signature—is a sign of the unphilosophical, unless perhaps it is plainly marked as an escapable diversion. And suppose now, instead of pursuing the sense of antagonism, or resignation, apparently depicted in this passage of the turned spade, we take in the fact that the passage is given an autobiographical presentation, enforced by a self-image of a teacher (in my quarrel with, or alternative to, Saul Kripke's reading of this passage, in my *Conditions Handsome and Unhandsome,* I call it a scene of instruction). More particularly, it is an image in which the spade may be taken as a figure for a writing implement—not in itself a very original idea perhaps (another elaborated instance of it occurs in the chapter "The Bean Field" in *Walden*), but heightened here by the connection with the hardness of the ground, hence with cultivation, and the limits of cultivation, as the destiny of the implement. It took years of experience in graduate school before I could quite recognize the degree of nervous laughter or outright contempt such a reading can elicit quite generally among teachers and students of philosophy, a degree well beyond a response to ordinary incompetence or inconsequence. I am saying that I still do not believe that this excessiveness is understood. Things get worse. My way of taking the passage shows it, more particularly, as a comment on a certain style of writing—evidently that of the *Investigations* in which it appears—since the implement is, to speak with due banality, masculine, but the gesture (of waiting, putting one's self, or body, on the line that way) is feminine; so that patience, and a recognition of rebuff and exhaustion, also become earmarks of the writing of this pedagogy, simultaneously with what Thoreau calls the labor of his hands only, and what Emerson in "Experience" calls manipular attempts and expresses impatience with. (This certain style and the importance of defining it is discussed in *Conditions Handsome and Unhandsome* under the title of the commitment to philosophical authorship incurred in the dimension of moral thinking I call there Moral Perfectionism.)

A counter-response, supposing that we are past derision and contempt, is to be expected: "If this is what Wittgenstein meant, why did he not say so? Aren't you reading more into the words than is there?" Instead of all the obvious answers we might give to what may be an intentionally obvious question, I note merely that wanting Wittgenstein to say something else is refusing to let him present himself as a (gender-complex) author who is, precisely, willing to show himself exhausted of reasons yet not necessarily therefore exhausted of patience. (What could he say that would better express his slight air of dissociation, his embarrassment at having his life called all at once into consciousness, than his noting an inclination to say something that strikes him as useless to say?) If what else or more he is to say is that he is not attempting to coordinate the pupil, bring him or her into line (as in Kripke's picture of the scene), but patiently awaiting a further response, are we to understand this as a promise to back his words on some later encounter? But this is nothing; he may be dead when the time comes, or as good as. What I want to know is whether he is backing them now, while I encounter them. And that knowledge is up to me.

Something his words await is for the student or reader (but which one, the one absent in the text or the one present to it?) to intervene, to ask something of them, an interrogation to match their arrogation. This is perhaps why the words have stopped some place. When to stop, how to end, is what the teacher cannot be taught. The distance from arrogation to interrogation is not understandable as prorogation, which is to say, as deferral; because to prorogue is to know how to begin again, or go on later, and we have no assurance of this when cultivation has stopped. Say that deferral or delay is what distinguishes the human, the crossover of instinct into reason. To interpret silence as delay—that is, to refuse to see that sometimes there is nothing to say—may be tragic. (This is a principal topic of my essay on *King Lear,* "The Avoidance of Love," a text that will come up in the next essay.)

What was I banking on in reading to such effect?—knowing the hard feelings it may cause, feeling sometimes that I would be glad to be free of the manner if I could. I know it has something to do with what I want of philosophy, or what I take philosophy to demand, in the first place to be inherited, mine to bequeath. Sometimes this drive of reading will present itself as taking away an author's breath, not taking away the right to speak, but following the inspiration otherwise than we find it followed; the author may or may not be glad. And is this, in each case, greedy or generous? In neither is it reading something in.

I am reminded, and will be reminded again, of an astounding confession of John Stuart Mill's in the third chapter of his *On the Subjection of Women,* a moment that reveals the essential autobiographicality of that text as a whole. Mill is asking, in effect, where his evidence lies for his conviction that women are the equal of men in intellectual originality, given their fewer numbers in the historical lists of intellectuals. Having answered that women are not in general trained to put their ideas in institutionally correct forms, that in other words their lack of numbers in certain institutions is determined not by their lack of ideas but by the constructions of those institutions, he goes on: "Who can tell how many of the most original thoughts put forth by male writers, belong to a woman by suggestion, to themselves only by verifying and working out? If I may judge by my own case, a very large proportion indeed." It is a vision of a very large proportion of high Western culture as plagiarized, speaking with voices other than those it owns. (This is not the same as the indictment that the culture has not listened to women; it is the indictment that it very conveniently has.) It is an autograph sign of that culture that when Mill, in the dedication of *On Liberty*, names Harriet Taylor as "the inspirer, and in part the author, of all that is best in my writings," he is not—any time I have heard the book mentioned—taken seriously. What can one confess?

It is as much or as little an answer to the question why I read and write as I do to say that I crave philosophy, as it is an answer to the question why I crave philosophy to say that I read and write as I do.

This takes me to my narrative: An image from which someone is missing, a figure whose mood is ambiguous as between action and passion, and whose recent halt and silence suggest abandoned cultivation, and whom to fail to understand or read presents itself as a failure to ask a saving question—such an image, I mean one so read, is one I can adopt as capturing my early sense of my parents' sense of me. I knew before each of them found ways to tell me—my mother in virtually so many words, my father in parable—that I was mysterious to them, which I suppose dominates my sense of their mystery to me, something that is evidently still living.

∼

Since I grew up in a couple of provincial capitals—Atlanta, Georgia, roughly from the mid-1920's to the mid-1930's, and in Sacramento, California, on and off from then to the early 1940's—it is perhaps not surprising that my mother, the product of a musical family, was not merely a very good, professional pianist, but that she was the best pianist I had heard until I went to college at Berkeley to major in music and learned, from the high musical culture of the yet larger provincial region of San Francisco, not to my complete provincial surprise, that there were other virtuosi living lives of local fame. In my rapidly increasing sophistication, what genuinely surprised me was to realize, acquiring means to measure it, how extraordinary a musician my mother was. My new acquaintances were educated—they knew opus numbers and could phrase Mozart and recognize that the words of the

songs of Schubert and Schumann and Brahms were set to words themselves to be contended with, and knew, beyond, some developments of
new music; but none could reach past what I still think of as my
mother's natural talent (though I knew that she had been well trained,
as if by chance, by a German refugee in the small music conservatory
in Atlanta in the years before the First World War, and encouraged daily
by her father), a talent gaudily attested in the assured fire with which
she played, for example, the Liszt Sixth and Thirteenth Hungarian
Rhapsodies, the closing pages of the Chopin First and Fourth Ballades,
or the Shultz-Evler arrangement of the "Blue Danube." What was truly
legendary about her playing, however, was her uncanny ability to sight-
read. It was this ability that meant, through the years of the Great
Depression, that if one musician in Atlanta was employed it was Fannie
Segal, whether for vaudeville, or for silent movies, or at the radio
station, or for high-society musicales in unapproachable mansions perhaps barely visible from the road, or for the traveling Yiddish theater,
or for visiting celebrities who suddenly needed a rehearsal pianist or a
substitute accompanist for a performance. (At my mother's funeral,
forty years after she had given up her musical career—for reasons that
still do not add up for me—the rabbi, long retired but called upon by
old ties for such occasions, remembered in his eulogy that young Fannie
had, in the course of the same year, his first with this congregation,
accompanied both Caruso and Cantor Yosele Rosenblatt.)

But I am talking about my image of this reading, my interpretation
of this woman's ability to bring to life whatever notes were put before
her. It was precisely not to my mind a knack of interpretation, but
something like the contrary, a capacity to put aside any interference, as
of her own will, and to let the body be moved, unmechanically, by the
mind of those racing notes. The lapse of distance—say that she was the
music then and there; there was nothing beyond her to read into—is
captured in my mind by an image of a certain mood that caused her
to play the piano for herself. Its scene was one I remember entering
perhaps three times in my life, coming home from school in the late

afternoon, a room darkened below the level at which reading was possible, having heard perhaps some meditative passage of Chopin before I opened the apartment door. It was highly unusual for her to be home at that hour, and asked about it, and about why the lights were off, she said it was migraine. I understood it as some kind of melancholy. If I was to inherit her world of music and of reading, was I to incorporate this mood, one in which she must remember her inheritance of this world, which meant the glamor of the precocious and the exceptional shown her privately, by her family and friends, and the honor of the compliments paid her as her musical adventures demanded public notice, but which also meant, given the mood, being absorbed by its disappointments? I sometimes measure this disappointment by the hope in Emerson's avowal: "I know that the world I converse with in the city and in the farms, is not the world I *think*." It happens, speaking of adding things up, that I am in the late stages of a project to define a genre of film I call the melodrama of the unknown woman, an essential feature of which is a woman's knowledge of a world against which the one she is offered appears second-rate. Most of the time I felt I knew in which world my mother thought I took my bearings. But when she took refuge in hers, there seemed no further room.

My father's contribution to my expectations of reading were, on the contrary, feats of a certain kind of interpretation, functions of his being known as the best teller of Yiddish stories in our small circle of friends. A characteristic genre of his favorite jokes concerned precisely scenes of interpretation, of the sort an immigrant community would have been painfully familiar with, often associated with trouble compounded by an ignorance of the law. A famous one concerns an old Jew taken before a judge for allegedly stealing a chicken, which begins with the judge asking for a translator; when a brand new lawyer, clearly a source of pride to his family, offers himself, the judge requests: Ask the old man whether he stole the chicken. In Yiddish the lawyer asks and in Yiddish the old man replies, in mighty and righteous indignation, "I

stole a chicken!?" The educated and properly-behaved lawyer turns to
the judge and reports, in English, "The old man says that he stole the
chicken." And so it goes on through mounting exasperations. My father
was of that school of story-telling that never introduced a story merely
as entertainment, but unfailingly also as morally pertinent to some turn
in a conversation. "Apropos" was my father's favorite high-class term
for this requirement.

Another of his touchstone stories—one of the ones whose lines
would be woven into family exchanges—is itself about pertinence,
dealing with matters of vocation or trade and tact or pitch. I set it down
here for future reference.

A modest congregation in a small town required a cantor for the
approaching high holidays and in the month preceding invited appli-
cants with good recommendations to conduct Friday night services as,
so to speak, auditions. It was clear among the elders almost from the
opening prayer that the first candidate would not do. Facing the
difficulty of breaking the news to the young man, the committee turned
to Shmuel, famous for his tact, to undertake the unpleasant task.
Pleased to be of service, Shmuel assured the elders that he would not
so much as breathe a word about the cantor's voice, or lack thereof.
After services the next day, he invited the young man for a walk, and
as they came to the edge of the neighboring woods, Shmuel gave out
a cry, grabbed for his foot, and just managed to hobble over to sit
himself heavily on a tree stump. He removed one of his shoes, held it
out to the candidate cantor, and asked him if he would judge whether
or not the trouble might lie there. The singer shrank from the request,
crying, "What am I, a shoemaker?" And Shmuel, with immense concern, let it out: "Well, and what else, after all, are you?"

I have known for some time that my fascination with Austin's practice came from its contrasts and its points of contact with defining
characteristics of each of my parents' salient talents. Austin too de-
pended in his thinking on a knack for telling stories with lucid pertinence to philosophical issues, often to moral dilemmas; and his

fastidiousness with the English tongue was an essential half of what my father despaired of for himself (eloquence was the other half), who possessed by the time I came into his life no ordinary language, his Russian and Polish fragmentary, his Hebrew primitive, his Yiddish frozen, his English broken from the beginning. It was familiarly said that the point of Austin's stories, those examples apart from which ordinary language philosophy has no method, required what you might call "ear" to comprehend (as in, more or less at random, setting out the difference between doing something by mistake or by accident, or between doing something willingly or voluntarily, carelessly or heedlessly, or between doing something in saying something or by saying something, or between telling a bird by its call or from its call). My mother had something called perfect pitch, as did one of her brothers. That I did not was a source of anguished perplexity to me, one of the reasons I would eventually give myself for withdrawing from music, particularly after I found that the only role I conceived for myself in music was as a composer. Yet I felt there must be something I was meant to do that required an equivalent of the enigmatic faculty of perfect pitch. Being good at following and producing Austinian examples will strike me as some attestation of this prophecy.

My parents took each other's talents seriously, more seriously than they took anyone else's that they knew; this element of romance lasted through their lifetimes. But they could never see reason in their despair of harmony, and their contrasts grew frighteningly polarized between his continuing rages (which I associated with what were called his attacks, from which he was sometimes reported as having passed out) and her periodic silences (in my experience, sometimes the effect, sometimes the cause, of the rages); between his contempt for the world and self-contempt for his failures in it, and her disdain for the world and for its ineffectual praises of her local successes in it; between the inexpressiveness of his wild love of the eloquence he would never have, and the glad unsayability of her knowledge of the utter expressiveness of music. The devastation of spirit in their quarrels, and their mutual destruction of interest in the world, are measures for me of arguments that must not be won, and hence—so I think—of my conception of philosophy as the achievement of the unpolemical, of the refusal to take sides in metaphysical positions, of my quest to show that those are not useful sides but needless constructions. Spending the bulk of my days alone, from the age of seven until the year before I went away to college, I from time to time thought that in their periods of locked speechlessness with each other, and with me, they were mad; and I wondered this about myself, in my absorption of their opposite griefs, becoming both their accused and their accuser, and as unintelligible to myself as if I had not learned speech.

A comparable isolation, and absence of voice, cloaks the teacher and the student to whom the teacher of the *Investigations* is inclined to say, yet refrains from saying, "This is simply what I do." It is such an experience that more recently has led me to sense the child in the quotation from Augustine's *Confessions* that opens Wittgenstein's *Investigations*—hence the child that recurs throughout the *Investigations*—as invisible to the elders among whom it moves, attempting to divine speech for itself, and as in a position of isolation and unintelligibility so complete as to reveal childhood as such to be a state akin to madness. (It does not seem irrelevant to me that it is the writing of two women, within the realm of publicly citable material, that I have adduced as attesting to such a perspective: Melanie Klein's descriptions of earliest childhood in terms of paranoid and depressive positions, and Elizabeth Bishop's autobiographical poem "Visits to St. Elizabeths," which presents images from a psychiatric ward in the form of a Mother Goose structure ("This is the House of Bedlam / This is the man / Who lies in the House of Bedlam," and so forth), so taking madness as playing to the death, but at the same time taking childhood as a madhouse.)

My first open recognition that I had my own knowledge of this condition, specifically of a sense of isolation more extreme than I could say, or felt could be told—a condition I knew that I had both to escape and to preserve—took the form, the summer after I graduated from high school, of a determination to change my name.

Some such impulse is no doubt an excessive variation of the excessive moment, normal enough in our roughly respectable circumstances, in which you know it is for you to leave home, as it were to find who your parents are, I mean what their mystery is. But this was 1942 and the world was not normal. I was sixteen, at the beginning of life's journey with scarcely a way to lose. In high school I had been the leader of its dance band, the first student to take that role, the faculty director having been drafted into the army—a nest of stories on its own but for the moment notable in its giving me a name, or description, without a future, the power to control the dance but at the price of not dancing. Put otherwise, even if the band had been good enough to try to keep together, almost everyone else in it was turning eighteen and waiting to go off to war.

Since my age then blocked that way of leaving home, I joined a dance band being formed by an alleged Latin American band leader who had come to Sacramento with a vocalist and an arranger looking for a pianist and a few other players before going on the road for the summer playing various resorts around northern California. In its small town, backroads way, it promised, and it has left, crumbs trailed from the skies of theater which the birds of oblivion have not found.

Outside the doors of all the ballrooms or night clubs we played that late spring and summer, the good-looking leader and his shining, distant singer (what had I to compare her with?) unfailingly had their publicity pictures well matted on the placard announcing the band and the hours of the nightly dancing. The inevitable slant at which the subject is presented in this genre of glossy, dramatically lit photo—the camera or its subject tilted just enough to indicate that the figure captured there is rather to be judged than to be judged by, to provide pleasure rather than mere instruction—is this work's angle of semiotic danger: missing the finesse of the concert artist's formal intimacy, it breaks with the formal rigor of the portrait only to risk a fall into the vague invitation of the shady. (My impression is that European and Latin American intellectuals can and perhaps must afford such an angle of self-consciousness, on the whole unlike their serious North American counterparts, who are so characteristically bound to an academic identity and its decorum.) Since the leader and the singer always had accommodations elsewhere than the rest of the band, I wondered whether they shared them. That wonder somehow, magnifying the general exoticism of this interlude, allowed me, among other adventures, to experiment with giving myself stage names. It was with names as I will find Rilke to say about the liberation of masks. And I knew as if at once, living in a medium of song, mostly of love songs, that the erotic was less a matter of encounters than of laws of encountering, or attraction, as Newton had shown. Sometimes the change of name felt like wanting to know what difference it would make if I did not simply announce my Jewishness by my name. Sometimes, and increasingly, it felt like a desire to know anonymity, as it were to have time to think, for a moment not to be on call. The tour lasted a couple of months and at its close the band, as planned, broke up. The leader phoned me some days later, offering me more money a week than, as it happened, my father was making to join him and the singer in Chicago as the anchor of a new band he was to introduce there in two weeks.

In the few days back at home in which I had to think over that offer, two new forces came into play. First, my parents reacted against the idea of my going on the road with a vehement unity and purity I had never known them to achieve before. (Had they, I wildly imagined, seen the singer, perhaps without my knowing it looked in at the band during its initial week playing at the de luxe hotel in town?) They became suddenly interested in my going off to college, a matter that had scarcely arisen for us (because of my age? because of the war? because the only focus of cultural or professional aspiration for me had hitherto turned on a life in music? because my parents knew nothing of college and mostly nothing about what others or their children did in Sacramento, which they always felt to be strange?). Second, I learned of a program the navy was announcing that could be entered at age sixteen-and-a-half, offering a college education with officer's training in return for signing on for (as I recall) a subsequent four years of service.

In the course of enthusiastically explaining this program to my parents I realized that they had interpreted some remarks of mine to mean that I had been contemplating trying to enlist in the army by lying about my age. That fear showed no knowledge of my repertory of daring. Running away from home to enlist in the navy was not part of it; enlisting the navy to help me leave home was much more like it. Moreover, my parents had evidently failed to consider that the consequence of a childhood accident—hit by a car as I ran headlong into our mostly uneventful street to retrieve a ball, I was left with a damaged left ear—might keep me out. I had already found out, from the latest doctor to treat one of my endless series of ear infections, that I almost surely would not pass the physical examination. But I convinced myself that this new navy program, since after all it clearly must be more interested in a good and malleable brain than in an unblemished body, was my chance to get into the war against Hitler. Since the band leader in Chicago was not interested in waiting the six to eight weeks it was likely to take to get an answer to my application, that path went unexplored.

But what had my parents' fears for what I might do, together with a damaged ear, got to do with my arriving at the possibility of legally changing my name? It may help to begin by saying why the change was from the given name Goldstein to the alias Cavell. Who gave the former and what is the provenance of the latter?

I was soon to discover that judges, not alone parents, need a reason to grant the petition to change your name, and a reason for the name you wish to change it to. In the judge's case, the need for a reason was related to the procedure I learned I would undergo of having my intention to change published in a newspaper every day for some weeks. The place in the one issue of the newspaper I was shown with my jeopardized name listed in it spoke of possible debts that the following persons may have incurred. Probably I did not sufficiently appreciate the irony in thinking what debts the law imagined a sixteen-year-old might have reason to flee from, but I began to know or know that I knew that the deed of declaring a name, or making a name, or any questioning of your identity, was being linked with criminality, forged together with it. Quite as if the reason for being singled out with a name were not just to be traceable in case of wrongdoing, but before that, as its ground, to serve notice that identifiable actions, deeds, the works of human beings, are the source of identity, and consequently constitute identity through accusation—all doing known as wrongdoing. The first guilt is being the one you are. So we are originally sinners. Hence, Emerson's defiant injunction—and following his Nietzsche's— to become, not simply accept, the one you are to be known as.

I have more or less been recalling Nietzsche's pale criminal as help in describing the beginning of my adolescent crisis—what the nineteenth-century philosophers of identity, or maturity, hence philosophers of adolescence, call youth, or the student (Emerson, Thoreau, Kierkegaard, Nietzsche). It will not be until well after coming to terms with the work of Austin (in particular, with the connection between his work on performatives and his work on excuses) that I will sense a workable articulation between Nietzsche's genealogy of the criminalization of individual injuriousness (as if all our actions are as arrows shot over the house, hurting brothers) and his perception of the creation of the human as of the creature with the right to promise.

I am sure I was not surprised that the judge, behind his gray columns and dark elevations, did not seem open to such reasons for change as my mad need for solitude and for getting to a say in my own guilts and promise. But I was surprised at the reason the lawyer my parents had retained managed to construct out of the mere information that I was planning to go away to college and that other members of the family had changed their name to something like Cavell. The lawyer said to the judge that there was precedent for granting the petition for a change of name to a minor who was going away to live with relatives. (It's hard now to think that there was no precedent for legally taking a stage name, but evidently I never mentioned the possibility, its having become within a matter of weeks as far-fetched to me as the fiction the lawyer had fabricated for himself.) Whether the judge believed the lawyer's story I do not know; or whether he feigned to believe, just possibly sensing—as by now I feel sure my parents sensed—that I would not be entering so extreme a request unless I were in that state I will long after find words for in the opening chapter of *Walden:* "Our moulting season, like that of the fowls, must be a crisis in our lives. The loon retires to solitary ponds to spend it." The linking of molting, crisis, solitude, and looniness is a condition of the moment of change I am depicting. My little book on *Walden,* as if more than twenty years ago establishing certain of the conditions of the present moment of depiction, comments on Thoreau's passage as follows: "What the imperative means ["our moulting season . . . must be"] is that our moulting season is not a *natural* crisis. . . . In the newest testament nature may prompt and bless my redemption; but it does not accomplish it on my behalf. What I have to work out is still my salvation, and still in fear and trembling. The crisis is still mine to spend" (*The Senses of Walden,* pp. 43–44).

But I was going to say why the molting produced the name Cavell. My choice has more than a touch in it of the myth of the secret name—even of radical propriety, of the name owned before the name is given, since one of the earliest pieces of family history told to me is that the name Goldstein was not the family's proper name but was dealt it by an immigration officer on their arrival in New York in 1905. According to the dates my father knew for himself, he was then also about sixteen when he got a new name, as my older son is now sixteen as I have come to the chance to tell this story, in his presence, for the first time publicly. (I once asked my father, since I had learned that records in his shtetl were by modern standards imprecisely kept, how he knew the date of his birth. He told me that when the immigration officer asked him for his birth date, he replied that it happened to be that very day. He smiled brilliantly as he told this, perhaps because it was true, perhaps because it was the first of an unfinished sequence of pertinent tales he would offer America, perhaps because he improvised it then and there for me. In any case I did not question the story then, and I have since said to myself that while receiving his new name, the one he gave me, was not my father's doing, he did give himself a new birthday, a rebirth brought forth for the new nation.)

The propriety I spoke of in the name I constructed for myself, a furtive legitimacy, began in one of those enigmatic remarks to which my parents were given. We had recently arrived for the first of our three two-year sojourns in Sacramento. It was 1935, a date colored in America, among other things, by its participation in the remarkably named Great Depression. My father's various tries at making a living from a succession of jewelry stores in Atlanta and in Miami had come to nothing. Hearing of this, the adventurous one among his brothers, who had made his way West while the rest of his family had settled either in New York or in the South, offered my father a job in his pawn shop, by far, it turned out, the most prominent and successful in Sacramento. As my parents and I were walking on a side street to that store, through the strange small town where boys my age were dressed in blue jeans, my father suddenly stopped to stare at a large plate-glass window with well-designed lettering spanning its area, and cried out with astonishment, "That's our name! Cavalier!" I gradually made it out that the largest of the letters on the window, forming an arc rising from its lower left corner to its lower right, spelled out this name; but even in my recurring phantasm of that moment, I have trouble seeing the letters forming one word. Perhaps interpreting my uncomprehending expression as doubting his claim, my father continued, "Cavalerskii [or Cavaleriiskii?] It's the same." (I still guess at the spelling, having yet to see it documented, either in family papers, which I was told were lost, or in what might remain of their shtetl a few miles from Byalistok.) In my later ecstatic improvisation, erasing and transfiguring my identity,

I took the first two syllables as more fittingly reticent than, and again different from, the first three (which was the form adopted by those other family members). Whatever escapes I was frantically contriving, I have from then on taken it as an obligation with each new acquaintance to let my origins show—not of course as if they were in doubt or as if they mattered to the other.

Freud famously claims that often a dream, even when thoroughly interpreted, has a navel, a spot where it reaches down into the untraceable complexity of the real. I would like to come close to the navel of my dream-action of changing my name—after a lifetime of associated tasks—but I leave it for the moment marked with the following memory. My father had, unprecedentedly, come alone from Atlanta to see me while I was still teaching at Berkeley, on learning that my first marriage was failing. As he and I sat in my newly rented, raw apartment, I felt his devastation begin to look for words of destruction. I said in effect: "Don't, for once, start this. You don't know what there is to be apoplectic about. I would rather live here, in these two rooms, than in your apartment that I have never called home." I realized that I had never before seen words simply fail him, instead of suffocate him. Letting him know that his guilt and sympathy toward me were misplaced was the beginning of my forgiving him. I was at once rewarded. We talked more than we ever had about the two families, his virtually a generation older than my mother's (my father, himself ten years older than my mother, was among the young ones of seven siblings, my mother next to the oldest of six); his father an observant orthodox Jew who lived past the age of one hundred, her father a secular socialist who died young; his family serious and mostly successful, socially and professionally, before whom he kept his loss of faith to himself; her family artistic, playful, mostly unsuccessful, before whom she was dominant, having been her father's favorite child and the best musician among them. When, later that afternoon, my father was gathering his things for the return flight to Atlanta, he asked, "What do you want?" I found myself answering: "To put together the Segals and the Goldsteins." "It's too much," he said. I felt the seriousness and sincerity of the moment, as if it contained the reason for his having made the trip. We were forgiving each other.

Certain questions of ear that run through my life—questions of the realities and fantasies of perfect pitch, of telling pointed stories, and of the consequences of a scarred tympanum—become, in these pages that record fragments of that life, questions of the detections of voice. But while the story of my ear as an organ of my body is less articulated here (for example, details of the primitiveness and painfulness of the early medical treatments of my ear, in the days still preceding the discovery of sulfa drugs, treatments which determined a general attempt to learn a distance from my body and so attempts to undo that learning, and which will mold the common male doubt, at certain stages, that one specifically will bear up under torture), it colors the others, in ways I know I have not fathomed. I mark this, before taking up the trail of philosophical texts drawn into the aftermath of the change of name and the harm to the ear, by pausing to tell the outcome, and something of the process, of my application to the navy officers' training program, to give some sense of the set of equations this application was simultaneously to solve. These events fill the latent days in Sacramento after the end of the tour of the summer resorts.

From the February I graduated from high school, suddenly informed in the middle of the school year that I had collected all requisite credits, I spent my nights as a working musician. Most of these nights I played piano in a commercial band of the kind that I went with on the road the following summer, strictly for the money and the occupation; but on incomparably the more significant, though rarer, of them I played lead alto saxophone in an otherwise black swing band, the biggest and best swing band anywhere near Sacramento, playing music so advanced, in addition to its advanced racial mixture, that it was unhireable. My days I spent working in my uncle's pawn shop, and then in my father's, when, to his great relief and even greater shame, he was able to start his own. I have spoken of my mother's life in another world; no one could have wanted out of the position my father's had come to more than he did. When I think, for example, of the day he had the store windows painted with new signs, seeing to it that its identification as a pawn shop was virtually hidden from the street, the fact that he acceded to my change of name seems almost understandable.

In my incorporation of his shame of himself, when was there time for mine of myself, and for mine of him, and for his of me? Suppose that I once recognized King Lear as ashamed and saw the tragedy in his loving daughter's effort to protect him from knowing it; and that I correctly saw that Emerson's incorporation in "Self-Reliance" of Descartes's "I think therefore I am," the philosophical discovery of self-consciousness which is to give us our last chance to prove our existence, was to challenge that chance, and instead to prove that we have become ashamed of our existence and are unable to know and prove it, leaving us to haunt the world. I can see that my clinical issues may have enabled a couple of critical insights here. But what does it take for the critical to inspire the clinical—in this instance to see that the trial of an ancient king and of a Concord sage may bear on the tribulations of an awkward sign at the back of a pawn shop window?

I indicate the fatality of matters I am having to pass by here by noting my primary responsibilities in both my uncle's and my father's pawn shops, namely, the writing of pawn tickets and the writing and delivering of daily reports for the police describing every article received, since some will have been reported stolen. Both tasks were shaped by printed forms, and toward the end of the last of the summers I spent at these works I remember saying to my father that I wanted a week free of them before school began again, since writing pawn tickets and reports for the police was not exactly what I had in mind, and probably not what the school sought, as serious writing. I regarded myself then as being amusing, but I lived to ask in what respects—say, in the demand for referentiality and in the fastidiousness of its audience—serious writing differs. It would please me if this present writing proves worthy of the question.

Opening his shop was made possible by the all-too-familiar fact that economic conditions boomed with the war and Sacramento became the beneficiary of several new and expanded air bases with their accompanying industry. The presence of the extraordinary group of musicians in the swing band—more talent than a town that size under normal circumstances could expect to support—was the result of their each having reason to move there to take military exemptions by working in war-related occupations; the several players I knew best had families and were, I judged, an average of ten years older than I. My introduction to them came through the pawn shop, with its (justified) reputation for honesty, and its stock ranging from bargains in diamonds and gold to buys in amplified guitars.

Some day I must describe what it meant to play lead alto saxophone with such a group; but privileged as I felt by their acceptance of my playing, I was at a different place in a different life, and I was looking for a way to scheme my way into the military. This was in early 1943, the war was still not going well, and I somehow figured that if I could get past the age barrier the damaged ear might be overlooked. For the navy's early-entry officers' training program, the initial hurdle was a competitive set of intelligence and achievement tests; I was successful, and the next step was the physical examination, which I was within a matter of days notified to appear for at the naval base in San Francisco. On the two-and-a-half hour train ride there, things began to seem suddenly quite real, and I hit on a plan for what to do when the ear doctor looked doubtful.

All my predictions came true. With a glance in my ear the doctor said, "Go home, son," and I began playing my hand. I said that I knew the inside of the ear looked strange, and was even hard to see, but suppose I could get a letter from my family doctor saying that he has treated the ear most of my life and that he knows it never gets worse than it is now. Wouldn't that reassure him? He agreed that it would. What had put such a thought into my head was that a cousin of my mother had run away with a gambler from San Francisco and my parents and I would see the pair from time to time on excursions from Sacramento. I didn't positively know that the gambler did anything illegal, but I phoned him, told him the story, and asked for the name of a doctor who would tell this lie about my ear. He knew one, not far from the naval base, and by the time I arrived at this doctor's office—dizzy with an excitement edged with a sense of the illicit—the letter was waiting. The navy doctor, on my return, accepted it.

As I was expecting congratulations and preparing to sign up, I was told to proceed to a room upstairs for an interview. My confidence and inventiveness vanished. On entering the room to find a group of some twenty men, most of them in naval officer's uniforms, sitting along three sides of it with a single empty chair at one end, I felt lost; and when someone asked, "What do you want to be and why should the navy support you?" all that occurred to me was that music was not a pertinent answer. In the face of an utterly predictable question, to which there were countless acceptable answers, I was struck dumb. It was another year and a half before I turned the age at which the army called me in for my induction physical, but for whatever reason the ear doctor on that occasion was uninterested in my offer to obtain a letter explaining the situation, and I returned to college.

The few people who knew this story, or parts of it—the gambler, certain friends of my parents—attributed the navy's rejection to anti-Semitism, a familiar charge about the navy in those years and moreover the running explanation or warning on my father's side of things throughout my life in response to various unhappy events. But on my mother's side a successful uncle liked to say: "There's no problem of anti-Semitism. Just be three times better than the other guy and you've got just as good a chance to get the job as he has." My own feelings in the present case were that if I hadn't been so isolated and ignorant of the world beyond playing music and writing pawn tickets and trying to escape quarrels that were meant to have no ending, I would have known about that interview and been prepared to talk my way through it. A very American response perhaps, and I came to an American conclusion—that I needed to become anonymous, go somewhere else, and begin again. How this did and did not happen is the general burden of what has happened since then, and of what will happen here, in the few texts of commentary there is reasonable time for me to adduce.

～

A passage from Emerson's "Self-Reliance" has struck me as a reading of my wish to construct a third name as a shelter from a given two. Emerson is there, as often, chiding our self-distrust, our discounting of the sentiments that are perhaps alone ours and can alone give our opinions substance. He recommends a figure to our attention:

> The nonchalance of boys who are sure of a dinner, and would disdain . . . to do or say aught to conciliate one, is the healthy attitude of human nature. . . . Independent, irresponsible, looking out from his corner on such people and facts as pass by, he tries and sentences them on their merits, in the swift, summary way of boys, as good, bad, interesting, silly, eloquent, troublesome. . . . But the man is as it were clapped into jail by his consciousness. As soon as he has once acted or spoken with *eclat* he is a committed person, watched by the sympathy or by the hatred of hundreds, whose affections must now enter into his account. There is no Lethe for this. Ah, that he could pass again into his neutral, godlike independence! . . . He would utter opinions on all passing affairs, which being seen to be not private but necessary, would sink like darts into the ear of men, and put them in fear.
>
> These are the voices which we hear in solitude, but they grow faint and inaudible as we enter into the world.

It is upon entering the world that we are given Lethe (as Emerson will note explicitly a few years later at the opening of "Experience"), and there is, as it were, no antidote for it, on a certain understanding of where to seek one. There may yet be a counter-gift, a way of remembering who or what you are before you are known to the world, accountable. If solitude were found in being alone empirically, why would the figure of the boy or the youth (as beloved as the figure of the reader by Thoreau and by Nietzsche as by Emerson) contrast with the grown-up social state of deafness to one's voices? The boy's independence blatantly does not depend on his being empirically alone. He has not yet relinquished his right to judge the world, passed from his neutrality, from the power to say no to false alternatives (sometimes called binary oppositions). Emerson's passage does not say that the boy's judgment is the best, or to be taken as final—that, for example, his limited experience is the soundest basis for judgment. It implies rather that the man's subsequent experience, become fixated, finalized, is no basis at all for judgments of his own.

Emerson's phantasm of the nonchalant boy as sure of a dinner is of one—while aware of the hundreds—who is still to make what he can, however he must, of *this* mother and father, so of their affections of sympathy and hatred. The idea of neutrality as an achievement is of one in recounting one's past, in which "trying and sentencing" the passing of people and facts into your world pretty openly says that you are to find your language, your own names, for what strikes you as good, bad, interesting, silly, eloquent, troublesome. This neutrality—this saying no to both, to the binaries of parental words—will find further interpretation when in a moment we take up what Nietzsche, after Emerson, calls becoming what you are (the subtitle of *Ecce Homo*, evidently taking up "the courage to be what you are" from Emerson's "Considerations by the Way," unless each is taking on a common predecessor). Thoreau pictures this as living wherever you are, something he describes in effect, or allegory, as writing that life, which is as much as to say, autobiographizing, signing the world.

That finding your neutrality is finding the language for becoming what you are before you are named for the world, is how I would have taken over Emerson's words when a few years ago I portrayed Hamlet as in a struggle not to be born, as if what he cannot forget (the ghost draining him of Lethe) means that he cannot have entered the world. I reported Hamlet's failed efforts at his task of neutrality (in his case, the failure to decline to take a revenge that was not his to take, against a mother's choice it was not his to unmake), in the following terms:

The father's dictation of the way he wishes to be remembered [asking the son to make his life come out even for him, so that he, the father, can rest in peace] exactly deprives the son, with his powers of mourning, of the right to mourn *him*, to let him pass.

Shakespeare's *Hamlet* interprets the double staging of human birth—which means the necessity of accepting individuality or individuation or difference, say one's separateness [I could not yet say one's neutrality]—as the necessity of a double acceptance: acceptance of one's mother as an independent sexual being whose life of desire survives the birth of a son and the death of a husband, a life that may present itself to her son as having been abandoned by her; and an acceptance of one's father as a dependent sexual being whose incapacity to sustain desire you cannot revive, which may present itself to the son as having to abandon him. Hence the play interprets the taking of one's place in the world as a process of mourning, as if there is a taking up of the world that is humanly a question of giving it up. (*Disowning Knowledge,* p. 189)

Hamlet's manic despair of making himself intelligible, telling his own story—in a world of fantasies inherited as rumors of origins (perhaps represented as fantasies poured into the porches of the ears, as Jean Laplanche and J. B. Pontalis almost put the matter), and in a mood of incomplete, suffocated mourning—may well suggest that establishing legitimate succession, the right to exist, is a function of a devious, staging knack for catching the conscience of authority.

This way of formulating the birth of the human is the product of two figures or scenes of inheritance that have recurred in my thoughts since my decision to incorporate autobiography into these lectures: the child in Augustine's account of his acquiring of language, with which Wittgenstein opens his *Investigations,* and—I guess the most famous of our texts of inheritance—Jacob's presentation of himself for Isaac's blessing.

When I earlier invoked the figure of the mad child I cloaked him as perhaps invisible and, as lacking language, lacking the means of making himself intelligible or, as Augustine remembers it, expressing his desires (beyond his needs). These predicates—or absence of predicates—I associate with my further sense of the child as in the position of having to steal language from his or her elders. The concept of stealing was prompted, I think, both by wanting to mark the absence of linearity in the order of words acquired, and by wanting to emphasize the asymmetry of work to be done on each side of the inheritance, the elders exaggerating their individual contributions of sounds, as if to relieve the anxiety in the fact that they mostly repeat themselves and wait, and talk to the air. This condition is the basis and parable of the possibility and necessity in the education of humans, of making language mine, of finding my voice (my consent, my right to speak, to promise, to break my promise), hence the standing threat of not finding it,· or not recognizing it, or of its not being acknowledged. Call this the question of plagiarism in human identity. It is the condition of possibility of the self-theft of culture that we saw John Stuart Mill confess on behalf of Western high culture. It is why what is ordinarily called plagiarism hurts as it does, as if there were a theft of selfhood, psychic annihilation; why it presents itself as vampirism. (The theft and reclaiming of a woman's voice is the subject of a genre of melodrama; it will come thematically into play when I consider the fact of opera. Those who are too sure ideas cannot be stolen like to say that ideas are not private property. But my feet are not my property, yet they are mine, and you are not to step on them. The punchline I have set up is not my property, but you are not to preempt it. My turn is not my property, but you are not to take it. Justice is not solely a measure of property rights.)

The further son, Isaac and Rebecca's Jacob, whom I bring in along with the infant Augustine, deviously taking language from us, I introduce as Isaac prepares to give his blessing, as Thoreau says we give everything, not without misgiving, famously musing: "The voice is Jacob's voice, but the hands are the hands of Esau." The puzzle for me—I cannot be the first to feel it—is how blind Isaac decides between the two forms of signature, by hand and by voice. Is he choosing the wielder of force over the possessor of words as the route of legitimacy? This hurts me. Is it that I can hardly bear the idea that the right to an inheritance is not given by reasons? Yet it is precisely when reasons are exhausted that authority is inclined to say, "This is simply what I do," namely, wait for the inheritance to be taken, overtaking the giving, treasonously. (Like forbidden pears.)

Yet I find I do not believe that a father can fail to know the origin of his son's voice, however at variance their accents. How can I doubt it when I might summarize my life in philosophy as directed to discovering the child's voice—unless this itself attests to my knowledge that it is denied, shall I say unacknowledged? What follows if we accept the fact that Isaac recognizes Jacob as he is displacing his blessing? Then he knows Rebecca's touch in preparing the ruse, and I suppose she knew he would know it. Is the idea therefore that he is granting her wish?—as if the true inheritor must have this wish? Or is the idea that the ruse or lure is a way of allowing the father to go against a traditional right (here, of the first-born) to the blessing and, without publicly breaking with expectation, to follow his wish?—as if the true inheritor must have this wish?

See what has happened to my thoughts of legitimate inheritance. They have led me to pry into the secrets between mother and father, wishing to overhear their communication, intercepting what I have elsewhere called their mind-reading of each other.

～

If writing philosophy is for me finding a language in which I understand philosophy to be inherited, which means telling my autobiography in such a way as to find the conditions of that language, then I ought even by now to be able to begin formulating some of those conditions. An obvious first is that a blessing has to be seen to be offered, a promise of an authorization for me to become what I am, which will be expressed as establishing my right to exist, to have a birth; a second, that the authorization is marked by the sense that I have arrogated the right to it, itself attested, third, by my having intercepted the conversation of my parents and translated their words by finding, fourth, a version of perfect pitch; and that this movement is, fifth, a process of passing again into my neutrality, which, sixth, bears testimony of the world I think. (To certify that these conditions are meant as provisional and exemplary, not as complete, I add another half dozen that may have been derived from my autobiographical reflections so far, and that I can anticipate in what I imagine will follow, whose concepts may receive parallel or transverse development: experience; conversion or rebirth; education; madness; uniqueness; not being understood.)

A way of assessing this set of conditions and of the idiosyncrasy of my derivations of its members is to note that all have derivatives in two remarkable texts that have already come up here, which may be understood as philosophical autobiographies: Nietzsche's *Ecce Homo* and Thoreau's *Walden*. I had thought that coming to terms with them would occupy the whole of this first essay, but now I can merely start steering toward its end by indicating the nature of their credentials.

Most obvious is, as noted earlier, their massive, insistent arrogance (as in Thoreau's "I brag for humanity" and in Nietzsche's "I have . . . given mankind the greatest gift that has ever been given it"), an arrogance associated with some remarkable experiences (in other autobiographies these might be conversion experiences or adventures of capture, in America by its Indians, in Europe by its own high culture), and associated with doubts that each exists among fellow human beings, doubts resolved ecstatically in something like new births, perhaps figured as the discovery of another world. Perhaps most significant for me, in claiming my inheritance of them here, is their registration of continuing parental interception. In *Walden*, in a passage of recently increased interest, it sounds this way:

> Books must be read as deliberately and reservedly as they were written. It is not enough even to be able to speak the language, the language of that nation by which they were written, for there is a memorable interval between the spoken and the written language. . . . The one is commonly transitory, a sound, a tongue, a dialect merely, almost brutish, and we learn it unconsciously, like the brutes, of our mothers.

The other is the maturity and experience of that; if that is our mother tongue, this is our father tongue, a reserved and select expression, too significant to be heard by the ear, which we must be born again in order to speak.

The opening chapter of *Ecce Homo* begins this way:

The fortunateness of my existence, its uniqueness perhaps, lies in its fatality; to express it in a riddle, as my father I have already died, as my mother I still live and grow old. This twofold origin, as it were from the highest and the lowest ladder of life, at once decadent and beginning—this if anything explains that neutrality, that freedom from party in relation to the total problem of life which perhaps distinguishes me.

Do we have measures for the intimacies and distances between these passages? Plucking out one plum we note that Nietzsche seems to be assuring his parents' separation by separating what is live from what is dead, and to be identifying his writing—that is, the life he is now alive to write—with his mother; whereas Thoreau declares his writing as of the father, and in such a way as to get his parents married, so securing his legitimacy, a status Nietzsche ostentatiously forfeits ("My time has not yet come, some are born posthumously"; "Why I Write Such Excellent Books" in *Ecce Homo*). But Thoreau goes on to balance his weighting of the father tongue, of writing over speaking, by in effect taking it back, that is, taking it further, and in the name of telling life from death: "The heroic books [written in the father tongue], even if printed in the character of our mother tongue, will always be in a language dead to degenerate times." And the proof that a language is alive is precisely that it becomes spoken by the living, the reborn—"not only read but actually breathed from all human lips"—though whether current human beings are alive or whether their living is a rumor (Thoreau likes to speak of those who are said to be living, say, in New England) is a recurrent enigma in *Walden*.

I observe that Thoreau's picture of an incessant struggle between writing and speaking, from which philosophy is born, contradicts Derrida's "[going] so far as to say," in "Signature Event Context," that the notion of writing as an *extension* of speech is "the interpretation of writing that is peculiar and proper to philosophy," to which he says he "[does] not believe that a single counter-example can be found in the entire history of philosophy as such." It is the interpretation according to which "the meaning and contents of the semantic message . . . [is] transmitted, *communicated,* by different *means,* by more powerful technical mediations, over a far greater distance, but still within a medium that remains fundamentally continuous and self-identical, a homogeneous element through which the unity and wholeness of meaning would not be effected in its essence. Any alteration would therefore be accidental." Whether you count Thoreau as a counter-example to philosophy's practice (that is, to the practice of philosophy "as such") is obviously a function of whether you count Thoreau as a philosopher (as such, or as self-declared). Since I do, I do.

And if Thoreau's view is allowed to counter Derrida's description of the philosophical dispensation concerning writing, it does so in each particular: writing appears in *Walden* not as an extension but as an experience of speech; its alteration of speech is not accidental but essential; it is not different in means or in medium if this means that you can tell the difference between writing and speaking by the senses as they stand, for reading with understanding requires reborn sensations, and first in hearing; and writing differs from speaking not by its more powerful technical mediation over greater distance but by a "memorable interval," which is to say, in Thoreau's lingo, by a discontinuous reconstitution of what has been said, a recounting of the past, autobiographizing, deriving words from yourself.

How important would this exception be? If Thoreau, along with Emerson, is a founder or finder of philosophy for North America, then this claim of Derrida's about writing contributes to that America's repression of its difference in philosophy. I put this so as to suggest that it is Derrida's fame, not necessarily what I therefore have to call his thinking as such, that contributes to repression. This is no small matter to get clear about. Philosophy's interpretation of writing, as publishing or broadcasting what is spoken, say, in philosophical dialogue, is bound to be a function of its interpretation of its esotericism.

Derrida, as is better known than I know it, relates philosophy's attachment to the voice to the scheme of Heidegger's reading of its interpretation of Being as presence. My second essay may have some bearing on this relation, but I offer, in advance of that, a speculation closer to home. I can imagine philosophy's esotericism either as supplementary to its relation to presence, or the other way around—either that philosophy originally interprets Being as presence and then explains the value and difficulty of transmitting this interpretation as its demand for esotericism; or contrariwise that philosophy originates in its refusals of sides, its quest for its neutrality, or autonomy, and explains this to itself as the esotericism of the knowledge of Being as presence. The relation, in either direction, suggests to me that Derrida's particular fame, because of his claim to inherit the classical apparatus of philosophical pedagogy, presents an enigma not presented by his famous compatriots with whose names his is commonly associated— Foucault, Lacan, Barthes, Lévi-Strauss, Artaud, Bataille, and so on— namely whether philosophy can be famous. It seems to me that for all Derrida's endless concerns with comprehensibility, he is very ready to express impatience and anger at evident misunderstandings of his writing, as if this presents no interesting philosophical question of his own draw to the esoteric. If so, this can have various explanations—that his mission to deconstruct philosophy's presence contains a twin mission to open up philosophy's esotericism, so that his willingness to see others as willfully misunderstanding, failing to try hard enough, is an intellectual and moral stratagem; or that he is clear about the differences between the polemical and the "philosophical" in his writing and that he wishes to repel, or annul, the title of philosopher. Nevertheless, his insouciance here, real or planned, is notable in view of his claim to inherit Nietzsche's *Ecce Homo* under his signature, a text, as suggested earlier, in constant question as to whether it has been understood.

The second half of Derrida's "Signature Event Context" contains his discussion of Austin on its subjects of voice and writing, a discussion I join in my second chapter. Here I need a word about Derrida's *Otobiographies*, about its stake in *Ecce Homo*, to make room as it were for the question of my own claims to speak for it.

Interweaving a degree of indirect discourse to achieve periodic confusion of tense and person, Derrida in his account of moments of *Ecce Homo* identifies Nietzsche's way of announcing his birthday as announcing his own. A sentence of Nietzsche's runs: "Not in vain have I buried my forty-fourth year today, I was *entitled* to bury it—what there was of life in it is rescued, is immortal." A sentence in Derrida's description of and commentary on the page on which this announcement occurs runs: "It is here: my forty-fifth year, the day of the year when I am forty-five years old." (That introductory "It is here" invokes the conjunction of the shifty "here" with Derrida's comedy at the end of "Signature Event Context" as he is mocking, not without respect, Austin's assurance about the uniqueness of signatures. We'll see.) It is perhaps my experience of the unfathomableness of the consequences for identity in adopting a name that alarms me about Derrida's gesture of incorporation. For example, to take a consequence unmarked by Derrida, Nietzsche's declaration in his announcement that he is *entitled* to bury his year itself has incorporated at least two prominent figures or scenes in which the entitlement to bury is contested: jilted Ophelia's illegitimate self-burial, which causes a controversy between church and state over the legitimacy of her communal burying (Nietzsche in *Ecce Homo* asks whether Hamlet has been understood); and Antigone's contested burial of her brother, leading to a joint immolation which displaces, or allegorizes, her wedding. Nietzsche's opening attribution to himself of, as previously cited, "that neutrality, that freedom from party in relation to the total problem of life which perhaps distinguishes me," seems a reasonable description of

Antigone's claim of distinction. Nietzsche is alive as his mother. That in incorporating another's identity you incorporate the identities that other has incorporated I might call the chain of identity.

My claim upon Nietzsche's autobiography is accordingly differently staged. With the other resemblances between *Walden* and *Ecce Homo* I adduce Thoreau's line, as he is about to recount in his opening chapter, the literal, or rather physical, ground-clearing for his house: "It is difficult to begin without borrowing." He notes, in this book of transcendentally faithful settling of accounts, that what he borrowed was an axe, which clearly enough figures the writing implement of one whose writing makes a house, hence one who criticizes, which is to say, cuts and separates, in order to edify; then this writing, in conjunction with the concept of borrowing, confesses its taking on of axes and issues explored and grounded by others. (This writer's account of his use of a hoe, namely, in cultivation of what he calls his field, is understandably different. Here he is for some reason even more explicit that the interest of it *is* the interest of its account, that is, its appearance in what became *Walden*.) Thoreau calls philosophy a field of economy, which is the basis on which, in identifying his book as the writing of an account of his economy—say, of his necessities and of the conditions or terms for meeting them—he is counting philosophy as autobiography. To show the power of Thoreau's use of the term "borrowing" would require showing its position in the perhaps interminable series of economic terms he casts into play in his opening chapter, entitled "Economy," perhaps beginning with two other of his terms for beginning, namely, buying and being given. And it would require making plain that the writer of *Walden* is taking on the meaning of borrowing as the root of burying.

I shall merely assert here that Thoreau's saying "It is difficult to begin without borrowing," as well as acknowledging the difficulties of acknowledging indebtedness, in its closeness to, and distance from, plagiarism, is a kind of repetition or anticipation of Nietzsche's gesture in celebrating his origins by burying something of himself. (When

Thoreau goes on to say of the borrowed axe, "I returned it sharper than I received it," he is perhaps borrowing that very thought from Milton's *Iconoclastes:* "For such kind of borrowing as this, if it be not bettered by the borrower among good authors is accounted Plagiare"—a quotation I borrow from a sourcebook through which I was checking the possibility that Thoreau had been borrowing something proverbial; perhaps he and Milton both were.)

Drawing this precautionary deed of an entitlement in or an incorporation of *Ecce Homo* is—to use a distinction drawn in the chapter titles of that book—not clever but wise. A writer compelled to invoke the case of Nietzsche for his or her work may feel compelled to take on, to bury in his or her own work, the dangerous fantasy of *Ecce Homo*'s opening identification of writing as possessing the power of death and the rescue from death. A danger of the fantasy lies in the knowledge that *Ecce Homo* is Nietzsche's last finished work, his last work of rescue, after which comes the decade of his madness. Is this the necessary continuation, perhaps always present, of the fantasy of philosophy's self-rescue, or was it only the empirical, accidental continuation, or discontinuation, of Friedrich Nietzsche's? I assume that no philosopher who has been brushed by the threat of skepticism can be sure once and for all on which side of this question he or she has enlisted, that is, sure whether neutrality has been achieved here. Taking my stake in Thoreau as my collateral for taking on Nietzsche goes back to the only other time I recall isolating a link between Thoreau and Nietzsche, in a passage in which I am rehearsing philosophy's threat of madness—a passage, I now find with some amazement, in which the concept of borrowing appears—and in which I speak of the bravery and in a sense the American luck of Thoreau's refusal of derangement (see *The Claim of Reason,* p. 469). (I link his American opportunity with his "[being] free of European quarrels," and I go on to express some reservation about what such freedom comes to.)

I am glad to have a more protected claim to Nietzsche's text, keeping the account balanced, mediated by Derrida's having used for *Otobiog-*

raphies, as the long opening epigraph for its portrait of Nietzsche's teaching in *Ecce Homo* (and a little in other texts), a sizable passage in the section "On Redemption" from *Thus Spoke Zarathustra,* beginning with the words, "for there are human beings who lack everything, except one thing of which they have too much—human beings who are nothing but a big eye or a big mouth or a big belly or anything at all that is big. Inverse cripples I call them." I assume that Derrida had not known—why indeed should he have? and should he now be interested to know?—that this sentence is one of those transcriptions Nietzsche characteristically makes of an Emersonian passage (or characteristically buries), this time from "The American Scholar," an early sentence setting up the essay's theme of the call for Man Thinking: "The state of society is one in which the members have suffered amputation from the trunk, and strut about so many walking monsters—a good finger, a neck, a stomach, an elbow, but never a man." Only the belly and the stomach overlap between these two writers' sets of body parts, but the giveaway conjunction is Nietzsche's description of the results as "inverse cripples" where Emerson has "walking monsters," both phrases that question the existence of humans by sensing a problem with their gait. (Is one to imagine that a phantasm of Oedipus and his limp is here accidentally associated with that of amputated members?)

Why, under what conditions, might anyone care about Emerson and Thoreau authorizing a stake in Nietzsche? I have argued enough, if insufficiently, over the years for Emerson's and Thoreau's characters of mind as philosophical, for their quality of intellect as equal to an inheritance of philosophy, for what that is worth; and for their position, still early by comparison with European time, as all but uniquely open to a responsiveness to both the German and the English traditions of philosophy, to that spiritual rift in the Western philosophical mind— argued enough perhaps to say what I think is lost when their thoughts are lost. Here, preparing words to say in Jerusalem, I am moved to reiterate two features of their texts that matter to me and that are even harder to credit, or perhaps to make intellectual plans for; features that in my fantasy nominate them as reticent, belated founders of some eventual international philosophical culture that will include both America (both hemispheres) and Israel—I mean their devotion to philosophy reaching beyond Christendom, beyond the West; and their problematic of the discovery of America (which for them has not happened), the problematic of what Thoreau calls "repeopling the woods," which is to say, making new people of these strange newcomers to this land, which proved not to be empty. These features are drawn, to my mind, in such a way that the human necessity of the quest for home and the human fact of immigrancy are seen together as aspects of the human as such. (One of Thoreau's terms for immigrancy is sojourning, another is rebirth; both are causes of his autobiography. One of Emerson's terms for it is abandonment, meaning both leaving and ecstasy; another is going onward.)

〰

Of the linked six or twelve characteristics or conditions I listed meant to demonstrate that philosophy and autobiography are to be told in terms of each other (that they are *not* to be so expressed hardly needs demonstrating; it is enforced), the feature of perfect pitch is apt to be the hardest to recognize, and the most variously or privately ratified. I mean it as the title of experiences ranging from ones amounting to conversions down to small but lucid attestations that the world holds a blessing in store, that one is, in Emerson's and Nietzsche's image, taking steps, walking on, on one's own. The attestation of one's autonomous power of perception may come in recognizing the autonomy or splendid separateness of another, the sheer wonder in recognizing the reality of the presence of someone whose existence you perhaps thought you had already granted. (It might come in the form of a new recognition of someone's text.) I think of the time my father related to the company at dinner that the Jews believe there is one moment in every twenty-four hours at which God grants a wish, and went on to say that he was making that wish at that moment of telling. I was most of all

amazed at how clearly I believed him, as if that had become a problem.
(I felt familiar with the fact that one could want something that much,
and familiar with my ignorance of what would make my father happy.)
And I think of the day my mother, working by then regularly in the
pawn shop, was asked by a young couple buying a plain wedding band,
awestruck by her emerald-cut diamond ring, whether it was real. (It
was the only possession, acquired late, and as a result of her work in
the store, apart from her Mason and Hamlin grand piano, acquired
early, and as a result of her playing in the theater pit orchestra, that she
took pride in; these were the only material objects in her life that were
not, it seems, fatally marked by her disdain for the second-rateness of
the world.) In response to the young pair she smiled a smile I knew
and answered, No. I still believe in the gift of her answer, that she gave
it that day without disdain for the question. I had, it seemed for a long
time, begun asking myself how these two human beings that I called
my parents, who were capable of these intensities, had nevertheless
come to their accustomed economy of life and death.

I close with an experience that assured me of an equivalent of perfect
pitch, of evidence of a world I think, at the limit of the world I had
conversed with—an experience of music, but one which, though ecstatic, did not lead me to ask for its blessing, as though the receiving
of it would not have become me, as though it were directed to a talent
not to a vocation, not to something I could deny as well as affirm.

The moment came in Ernest Bloch's music theory class, held two
hours every weekday in the late afternoon for six weeks the summer I
was a second-year student at Berkeley. He was in his mid-sixties, my
age now, and would sometimes tell stories of Paris around the turn of
the century when he was a music student roughly my age as I was
listening to him then. Sometimes he was moved by a memory to give
a demonstration of what conducting essentially consisted in, asking
what communication is, or what constitutes a cue; or he would cover
both long walls of staved-lined blackboards with different dispositions
of a C-major triad to warn against believing in simple or academic

definitions of harmonic correctness or of proper voice-leading; or he would interrupt himself to read an excerpt from Plato, or from Confucius, or—a recent discovery of his—from Stanislavsky; or he might move to the piano to play a passage from a Schumann string quartet referred to by an anecdote from the history of Robert and Clara Schumann related in someone's letters; and all in all he bespoke a world of aspiration so vivid, a life of dedication so extensive and so constant—as if a wish were being granted me every moment—that I would at the end of a class sometimes find myself having trouble breathing, and I formed the habit of walking immediately after each of its sessions into the adjacent hills for an hour or so of solitude, as if I had become too consecrated to touch. Well, well, what do you expect of the effects of the spell of an old master on a young man?—the pathos of the old heightened by his dissatisfaction with the degree of his fame and his disappointment with the new directions taken by the art to which he had given his life, the young wild with muteness, feeling for the first time intelligible, but to a world he at the same time somehow surmises not quite to be his.

It will take some years to discover another, but I knew from that time inescapably—not always hopefully—of the promise of some such existence. One of the exercises Bloch liked to introduce into his classes epitomized for me both the far shore and that it was not quite my direction. He would play something simple, at the piano, for instance a Bach four-part chorale, with one note altered by a half step from Bach's rendering; then he would play the Bach unaltered. Perhaps he would turn to us, fix us with a stare, then turn back to the piano and repeat, as if for himself, the two versions. The drama mounted, then broke open with a monologue which I reconstruct along these lines: "You hear that? You hear the difference?" His voice was surprisingly unresonant and sounded pressed with the labor of excitement, an exotic effect increased by his accent, heavily French, but with an air of something else. He went on: "My version is perfectly correct; but the Bach, the Bach is perfect; late sunlight burning the edges of a cloud. Of course

I do not say you must hear this. Not at all. No. But." The head lowered
a little, the eyes looked up at us, the tempo slowed ominously: "If you
do not hear it, do not say to yourself that you are a musician. There
are many honorable trades. Shoe-making for example." (Something in
me still believes that he and my father received funds of stories from
the same town.) I heard the difference; I suppose I assumed, without
evidence, that not everyone did. But I would come to hear something
more about myself in that drama; I would find that I was as interested
in the understanding of what I heard, as thrilled by the drama of the
teaching of it, as I was interested in the rightness and beauty of what
I heard; they were not separate. The assigned question of hearing, of
an ear, produced a private triumph, and spoke decisively, unforgettably,
of a world of culture beyond the standing construction of the world.
Yet I did not want this transcendence of culture to require a comparatively rare talent, even a competition of talents, in order to participate
in it. I began reading Plato, Confucius, Stanislavsky, as well as Schumann's criticism.

The trauma of the birth of culture in oneself, the sure knowledge
that there is a life of art and of the mind, that such a thing as intellectual
companionship exists, never, I provincially felt, dawned on an intellectually starved provincial with more impressively banal thunderclaps
than those I was being crushed and lifted by. Whatever conditions
preceded them, I date from that time a knowledge of the moral life as
containing a dimension or perspective of what I came to call Emersonian Perfectionism, one shared in by Nietzsche and Thoreau. It is a
perspective from which—given that there are choices we must make
between what is right and wrong to do and what is good and bad to
get—the given world is to be judged in which just these options and
objects with which the world is conversant make the world in which,
and in terms of which, to choose; a perspective from which it may be
seen that with a small alteration of its structure, the world might be
taken a small step—a half step—toward perfection.

It was not until Austin's semester at Harvard, to which I turn next, ten years after Bloch's summer at Berkeley, that I found elements of a voice in philosophy that might permit my participation in that perspective.

I said earlier that I identified with the perhaps absent, silenced child of Wittgenstein's parable of the turned spade, but yet no less with its present, silenced grown-up, who keeps himself or herself visible, waiting, with hovering attention. The continuation of that fantasy that I fear most, my idea of philosophical tragedy as it were, would be of the child returning with a question and I unresponsive, unable so much (it is very much) as to provide the assurance of my listening. It is the fear to be seen in old Lear, unable to bear his child's silence, unable equally to bear what she has, and has not, to say.

~ 2

Counter-Philosophy
and the Pawn of Voice

To Alexander Thomas Cavell Batkin

Benjamin transposes this conception further into the mystical [that is, beyond the merely empirical and institutional "secrecy" of the Hebrew name, as cited in the epigraph to Chapter 1]. Maturity, which for the Jewish tradition has a sexual character only marginally, is now related to the awakening of love, which can occur more than once in life, namely with each real new love. For the pious man, which is to say the man true to the Law, his "secret name" remains "perhaps" unchanged throughout his life, because apart from the marriage sanctified by the Law he knows no re-newed sexuality in reference to other women. For him, by contrast, who like Walter Benjamin does not count himself among the pious, the change of his name can reveal itself all at once with a new reaching of maturity, which is to say with a new love.

Gershom Scholem, "Walter Benjamin and His Angel," p. 217

The semester Austin came from Oxford to deliver the William James Lectures at Harvard, in the spring of 1955, he also offered a graduate seminar with the title "Excuses" and in addition held Saturday morning discussions with the philosophy faculty (which I and a few other privileged graduate students were invited to attend) on the subject of what was variously called empirical or perceptual certainty or knowledge. It was, I believe, Austin's forty-fourth year, and it would prove to have seen the bulk of the work associated with his name. The material on excuses is encapsulated in his paper "A Plea for Excuses," published the following year; his notes on performatives and those on perception were edited, and where necessary reconstructed, under the titles, respectively, *How to Do Things with Words* and *Sense and Sensibilia* and published posthumously half a dozen years later. The first practical result for me on encountering Austin's teaching was to throw away beginnings and plans for a perfectly good Ph.D. dissertation (for what it is worth the subject was the concept of an action in Kant and Spinoza). Perfectly good, oddly, means good enough to have earned the degree but not good enough to have given me what I variously imagined as a voice, a way, a subject, a work of my own. The depression in this decision to stop what I was doing was less magnified than it might have been in repeating that of my decision almost ten years earlier to put away my beginnings as a composer, because this time there was an associated exhilaration in clearing the ground.

Three springs after the one at Harvard, Austin spent a semester at Berkeley, where I had by then been teaching for a year and a half, so filled with the sense of the urgent value of Austin's contributions to philosophy that I became rather a nuisance about it in my classes and in conversations, and had been asked—assigned was rather more the speech act in question—to defend Austin in public at a colloquium at the Christmas meetings of the American Philosophical Association, against the criticisms of my accomplished colleague Benson Mates, who found the philosophical yield of Austin's work to be—not to put too fine a point on it—nil. When Austin arrived for his term with us some weeks later, and again arranged for weekly faculty discussions, it was agreed that an early session would be devoted to his own responses to Mates's Association paper. Having somehow already acquired a copy of that text, Austin asked me for a copy of my reply, by then tripled or quadrupled in length, and on the day of the discussion he placed the copies of both papers before him on the seminar table but would prove to mention mine neither publicly, in the discussion, nor privately afterward to me. It was my first serious philosophical essay and I interpreted the silence, painfully, as Austin's disapproval. Publication of Mates's and my colloquium had already been arranged and I had a brutal struggle with myself about whether to try to withdraw my contribution. The aftermath of this struggle lasted for some years, only reliably diminishing as I began to learn that Austin had recommended and assigned my paper when he returned to Oxford; only then did I recall that in his discussion with Mates Austin had started things off in the place and in roughly the spirit in which I had begun my paper, namely, with the conflict Mates had produced between Austin and his colleague Gilbert Ryle and with the series of questions I had raised to counter the conclusions Mates had drawn from the conflict. Then it dawned on me that a more obvious interpretation of Austin's silence was that he was establishing a private and sincere moment of acceptance of the work I had done. Perhaps I found this behavior too foreign, too formal or hidden, to take in at a glance; but I seem to have found it also too familiar to take kindly, since my reaction on hearing of his praise was anger: Just like my father, I told myself; public praise and private denial; somebody is crazy. My mother fairly perfectly reversed this economy, dealing in private acceptance of my high hopes, when she was unabsorbed, together with disdain for public assessments of those hopes. I think I may have come to conclude from this mismatch alone between my parents' economies of praise that it is quite impossible for me to be realistic about the degree to which any work I do can be known.

This might have remained a clinical problem, but it has entered for me, I can say sublimed itself, into the critical question of the writing of philosophy, most particularly into the ideal I have of eliciting philosophical conviction, according to which one becomes its addressee only to the extent that one imagines becoming its origin or sender, so that you accordingly realize that you are being told nothing, nothing exactly new. It is more or less understandably difficult to get credit for writing this way, say, unassertively, especially when the writing is at its most successful.

My defense of Austin against Mates's charges was reprinted as the title essay of my first book, *Must We Mean What We Say?* published some ten years after Austin's death. The summer of the following year, 1970, I was invited on the strength of that book to Paris, along with some other English-speaking philosophers, to meet a certain Jacques Derrida, with whose views, my host was interested to tell me, my book bore a number of affinities. One morning of the three or four days of scheduled conversation with Derrida was to be devoted to a discussion of my title essay, and as I entered the seminar room I noted my book in Derrida's hands. Again my exposed essay did not come into discussion, this time because no one present, so far as I could tell, besides Derrida and me, was much interested to think about Austin. The following year Derrida delivered what he names a communication, entitled "Signature Event Context," the second two of the four sections of which are a response to Austin's *How to Do Things with Words*. I became aware of this communication six years later when the first two issues of the journal *Glyph* came my way, the first containing a translation of Derrida's communication along with a reply from John Searle, the second containing Derrida's response to Searle, "Limited Inc."

Anyone *satisfied* by this encounter was, I felt, likely to be getting the wrong thing out of it, say, *Schadenfreude* at the ruinous results of the two traditions of Western philosophy looking up from their separate works. But the studied indecorousness of Derrida's reply to the sheer dismissiveness of Searle's reply, together with Derrida's intervening fame, launched the incident into a life of its own, more than filling the air in which an intervention of my own, recounting my sense of Austin's voice, might have found room to breathe.

I had in a way been prepared for Derrida's sections on Austin by the discussions of voice and writing in *Of Grammatology*, which I read in translation in 1977, with excitement, but with, I guess, equal disheartenment. It struck me, as "Signature Event Context" would strike me, as denying the event of ordinary language philosophy, as seeing it rather as, after all, a continuation of the old questions, the old answers, about which Samuel Beckett (or rather his character Hamm) had said, "Ah. There's nothing like them." Now of course that consequence, so serious for me, is only incidental for Derrida, an artifact of a bigger hunt. So I might be told, as elsewhere, that I take Derrida's denial too seriously. In the words of the Ophelia character in Hitchcock's *North by Northwest:* See what I mean?

I had just sent off to the publisher the manuscript of *The Claim of Reason*. If I had had then to give a one-clause sense of that book's reason for existing it might have been: "to help bring the human voice back into philosophy." That is the charter Austin and the later Wittgenstein assume in confronting their reader with their arrogation of voice, in all its ungrounded and in a sense ungroundable arrogance—to establish their sense that the voice has become lost in thought. It has become lost methodically, in philosophy's chronic distrust of ordinary language, arriving at some final crisis in analytical philosophy's unfavorable (in *Philosophical Investigations* Wittgenstein calls it normative) comparison of ordinary language with logical construction; and lost theoretically, in the conclusion of modern skepticism, whose advent begins (scenically in Descartes and in Hume) by taking the individual voice, or breath, away—as in Descartes's private and mad "astonishment" at what he has discovered about his impotence to prove his existence, or in Hume's anxious sociability, putting aside the everyday incommunicability of what he has to say about the failure of human knowledge. Derrida's assertion of philosophy's over-praise of the voice struck me as jamming my call for it.

The Metaphysical Voice

The voice Derrida finds over-praised, or over-counted, is not exactly the voice on which Austin and the later Wittgenstein pin their hopes, our unastonishing yet astonishing ability to say what we say, I for you, you for you. It has never been easy to articulate those hopes precisely.

In a brief memoir of Austin I published a few years ago I spoke of the revelatory effect his first classes at Harvard had on me. Like any conversion experience—any turning, however small, of a cheek, of a mood—the effect is apt to seem out of proportion to anything you might think to call its cause. Conversion (or as Emerson says it, aversion) is of its nature hard to explain, to others as to oneself. Could it really be that so decisive a change in the course of my life—let's even say it was merely, or only, or sheerly, or just, or simply (a favorite line of distinction of Austin's) a change in my intellectual or academic ambition or craft—could have been brought about by Austin's trivial, if amusing examples? *How* could it have been? I think of the quite indubitable differences he draws between shooting your donkey by mistake or by accident; of the differences between being sure and being certain of a color; of seeing bread and seeing the signs of bread; of our asking "How do you know?" not "Why do you know?" and of our asking "Why do you believe?" but in general not "How do you believe?" You start out—most do—thinking there can't be all that much difference between the similar phrases; then after a couple of Austin stories the difference becomes—for some—so lucid and so decisive that you shudder to think of your previous, torpid state of illusion. Eventually, though, more come to conclude that the state of illusion was after all Austin's, in his convictions of the ordinary, and not that of one's own conformity.

Austin's teaching was the occasion for me on which to ask, somehow differently from any way in which I had been able to ask it before, whether I was *serious* about philosophy—not quite as measured by its importance (to the world, or to my society, or to me), but as measured by a question I felt a new confidence in being able to pose to myself, and which itself posed questions, since it was as obscure as it was fervent. It presented itself as the question whether I could speak philosophically and mean every word I said. Is this a sensible test in choosing a career? Or even in choosing, or seeing that you have chosen, a friend? And does it mean that I have—before I speak—to ask whether I am sincere in my words, whether I want all of their consequences, put to no matter what scrutiny? Who would say *anything* under such conditions?

It has more than once been claimed—I hope mistakenly—that Derrida's encounter with Austin's text, and then, at much greater length, his exchange with Searle, represents the closest that the traditions of French-German philosophy and American-English philosophy have come to talking to each another in detail. Searle is a philosopher trained at Oxford while Austin was still alive, and his book on speech acts continues to be more influential, in both literary studies and in philosophy, than Austin's original work that invented the subject; it is my impression that the effect of his reply to Derrida has encouraged the suspicion (to say the least) in which Derrida's work continues to be held by so many professional philosophers, and not just within the English-speaking world of philosophy. At the same time Derrida's influence within literary studies has kept the image of Austin too much tethered to his theory of performatives, and within that theory, to the several citations Derrida found suitable to his own purposes for "Signature Event Context."

This confinement has helped perpetuate the thought that Austin underwrites some idea that language contains a general, unified dimension of effect that can be called one of performance or performativity, and that he advances a general contrast between ordinary language and literary language. These ideas alone are sufficient to destroy any contribution that Austin's distinctiveness might lend in such discussions.

My own feeling is that while Derrida found Austin philosophically interesting, even congenial, and Searle had found Austin useful and worth defending against Derrida's treatment of him, neither really felt that Austin's is a (philosophical) voice whose signature it is *difficult* to assess and important to hear out in its difference. If what either of them says about Austin's ideas of language is right, then my question of seriousness, forced upon me by those ideas, is not only difficult to articulate, but pointless. This is a way of putting the drift of my original defense of Austin, against Mates, that is, so far as Austin was pertinent to the American-English side of philosophy. Why my reasons have receded against trying to show this sense of pointlessness, or failure to hear Austin's difference, in the opposing case of Derrida, that is, from the French-German side of philosophy, I will not begin to say; but none of them, I think, is as important as considerations for now going ahead with the attempt. Generally, while many people now express relief that Derrida's influence is waning, that influence remains immeasurably powerful and, on my view, deserves a finer fate than its detractors wish for it, if perhaps not quite the finality that its admirers have traded on. Specifically, Derrida is right to have emphasized the fundamental importance of the human voice in Austin's work, and his "Signature Event Context," read so as to elicit answers from Austin's work, not as a criticism of it that is either omnipotent or incompetent, constitutes an acute and rare encounter concentrated on the interacting themes of voice, writing, and philosophy.

So that now, and here, in a chapter between a chapter on Western philosophy's arrogation of voice and one to come that is to consider the medium of opera, I would find it unbecoming of me not to say what I can directly about Derrida's encounter with my old teacher. I shall proceed in a sense with deviousness, but in a sense with maximum directness. To outflank what for my purposes would be perhaps distracting and certainly exhausting engagements, I am going to pretend that the controversy between Derrida and Searle did not happen—as in a sense each of them insists it did not—and speak to Derrida's words on Austin as if for the first time.

∾

Derrida's deconstructive objective is the metaphysical voice, I mean the voice of metaphysics, philosophy's hoard; whereas the voice Austin and Wittgenstein call on in asking their interlocutors to say what they say, to arrogate our voices if they dare, they call the voice of the everyday or the ordinary. They call it this—thus contextually defining what they mean by the ordinary—precisely to *contrast* their appeal with the appeal to metaphysics. The other running contextual definition they give of the ordinary contrasts, in a different spirit, ordinary language with formalized language (say, mathematical logic). (That in literary studies Austin's ordinary language is instead thought to be contrasted with literary language means to me that Austin has not there been received. This is not to be taken to mean that I believe he is sufficiently received in philosophical circles.) Derrida is every bit as opposed—of course in his way—to the metaphysical voice as Austin and Wittgenstein are. But he makes it his business to monitor and to account for its encroachments while seeming, or giving the impression to some that he means, to be speaking in it, no one more cheerfully. Austin, for reasons I must go into, believes, or gives the impression, that no serious philosophical account of it is possible, or required. Wittgenstein has a web of accounts or impressions of it, but it is not a web that suggests, as Derrida's does, its final overcoming, that is, that suggests that it will end philosophically.

Underlying the opposition to the metaphysical voice that I say Austin and Wittgenstein share with Derrida, there is all the difference between the worlds of the Anglo-American and the Continental traditions of philosophy, differences between their conceptions of and relations to science, to art, to culture, to religion, to education, to reading, to the ordinary. . . . While Derrida and Wittgenstein see metaphysics and the ordinary as locked in contrast, in Derrida, as differently in Nietzsche and in Plato, philosophy retains a given reality, an autonomous cultural, intellectual, institutional life, that in Wittgenstein is gone. For Wittgenstein and Austin, as for the figures of Socrates or Descartes (in the *Meditations*) or Hume or Emerson or Thoreau, the mood of philosophy begins in the street, or in doorways, or closets, anywhere but in philosophical schools; it is philosophy's power to cause wonder, or to stun— to take one aside—that decides who is to become a philosopher. To announce the question of the death of God was at once to announce the question of the setting of reason, as of the light of the sky, and philosophy becomes a clinical problem as much as a critical one. Since philosophy cannot have the grounding it seeks, perhaps it will find a cure or a close. Wittgenstein and Derrida differ in their standing within these expectations.

Since Derrida sees ordinary language as an "effect" ("Signature Event Context," p. 19) of a general writing, which is its possibility, and since Wittgenstein sees metaphysics as an effect of ordinary language, needing its words but denying their shared criteria, it should not surprise us that each pivotal concept at issue between Derrida and Austin—presence, writing, voice, word, sign, language, context, intention, force, communication, concept, performance, signature; not to mention, of course, consequent ideas of philosophy, of the ordinary, of analysis, of the end of philosophy, of work, of fun—is turned by their differences. I know of no position from which to *settle* this systematic turning, so I must hope that my writing about their encounter is sufficiently aware of the constant danger of begging their questions.

As a step into Derrida's "Signature Event Context" and to mark the rift of philosophical tradition, I excerpt some sentences from the last pages of one of Derrida's first principal works, *Speech and Phenomena: And Other Essays on Husserl's Theory*. Derrida's thoughts there evidently underlie those of "Signature Event Context," as that later communication moves from its opening two sections to the two on Austin. I take the sentences as touchstones of the estrangement between the traditions, that is, as registering that they bear to each other an intimacy as well as a distance, that they are halves of the same—that is, of the philosophical—mind. Husserl is a significant crossroads of this estranged intimacy since his discussions, for example, of the status of concepts, and of meaning in the face of non-references of language, and of the difference between the indicativeness and the expressiveness of signs, can be taken as made obsolete, in a sense unreadable quite seriously, by the different developments from Frege represented in the work of Russell's and the early Wittgenstein's philosophies of mathematical logic. Over the span of Husserl's work, the traditions of post-Kantian philosophy can be said to have become, beyond being incomprehensible or useless to one another, ludicrous to one another.

Here are the sentences on my mind from Derrida's discussion of Husserl's phenomenology:

> *Within* the metaphysics of presence . . . we believe . . . in absolute knowledge as the *closure* if not the end of history. And we believe *that such a closure has taken place*. . . . Absolute knowledge is the end of the infinite, which could only be the unity of the concept, logos, and consciousness in a voice without *différance*. This history is closed when this infinite absolute appears to itself as its own death. *A voice without différance, a voice without writing, is at once absolutely alive and absolutely dead.*
>
> As for what "begins" then—"beyond" absolute knowledge—*unheard-of* thoughts are required, sought for across the memories of old signs. (p. 102)

Because I am impressed by Heidegger's and Derrida's acquiring their signatures in part by writing in interpretation of Husserl, I feel the need for a measure of the scandal it represents that I read this text of

Derrida's on Husserl for the first time only in the course of drafting this chapter, in July of 1992, in preparation for the lectures to be delivered the following November, as if I could plan to assess it on, comparatively speaking, a moment's notice.

If I say that I put off studying the Derrida because I had not read much Husserl, this may seem a good excuse or a further scandal. Either reaction assumes a view, or refusal of a view, of the scandal of the rift in the philosophical spirit. In a little while I will be moved to ask how much Austin Derrida had read before composing "Signature Event Context," and how much specifically this matters; to ask, perhaps, in case he had reassessed Austin's *Sense and Sensibilia*, whether he had beforehand or collaterally pondered A. J. Ayer's *Foundations of Empirical Knowledge*. I would ask because *Sense and Sensibilia* is a book of notes that can precisely be described as a dismantling of the craving for presence and as proceeding in relation to Ayer's book as Derrida describes his *Speech and Phenomena* as proceeding in relation to Husserl's—namely, by "going *through*" that philosopher's text, by which Derrida says he "mean[s] a reading that can be neither simply commentary nor simply interpretation" (p. 88).

What is more, Austin and Derrida each explicitly take the work they are reading as exemplary of an entire tradition, and having constructed what each obviously takes to be an exemplary reading, each knows his own work to be in a new place, measured by his tradition, with no way back to the way of the old. (Theirs is not, or not just, the old way of argumentation and refutation, a way which may leave much of the original text standing, or else in need of replacing, but with its context, so to speak, intact.) Now a favored term or turn of criticism or diagnosis Derrida offers of Husserl's account of signs is to say that it excludes something as external or accidental to its subject that is, more patiently or accurately, to be seen as internal and essential to it. And this turns out to be the exact or precise criticism Derrida offers, repeatedly, of Austin's work on the performative utterance. For example: "Even while repressing difference by assigning it to the exteriority of the signifiers, Husserl could not fail to recognize its work at the origin of sense and presence. . . . But it was necessary to pass through the transcendental reduction in order to grasp this difference in what is closest to it—which cannot mean grasping it in its identity, its purity, or its origin, for it has none. We come closest to it in the movement of differance." I know accomplished thinkers who find such language as Derrida's here to repel all impulse to consider rational response. But some forbearance might reveal a comparison with a favored turn of Austin's (and Wittgenstein's), according to which philosophy stands accused of repudiating the language—call it, accordingly, ordinary—on which philosophy's own sense depends.

Indeed, Derrida's formulations in this passage seem especially clear for our purposes, so I spell out the moment a little more bluntly, if only to mark where I might be jumping off the track. If there were a pure origin of, let's say, epistemological authority—phenomenology seeks to reach it in its reductions; the sense-data or sensibilia theorists, whom Austin undertakes to dismantle, seek it in, let's say, a method of doubt—it would be a self-presence into whose unity a pure difference would have to arrive. If this self-presence would be, or presents itself (in fantasy) as, the exercise of the voice, and there is no such pure origin, then what there is "instead," closest to pure origin, is the movement of difference. Movement of difference is a definition of what Derrida names the trace; it is a feature of his new, nonclassical, picture of writing. This way of placing the origin of trace indicates how writing may be said to come "before" voice, as well as, classically or colloquially, after it.

But these writings and voices that precede and succeed one another seem to pose and to cross the same line that separates metaphysics and the everyday. Presumably they are meant to help chart that projected line. But to say with Derrida that the ordinary is the "effect" of the metaphysical seems an up-scale version of the academic answer as to how the thing-in-itself is related to the object of knowledge, namely, as "causing" it (whereas the concept of cause is confined by Kant to relations between objects). For Derrida the origin of the metaphysical voice is established by being broken; for Wittgenstein the origin of the quotidian voice is the return from the metaphysical. A trouble with Derrida's picture is that there never was a "way" to an origin; a trouble with Wittgenstein's picture is that there is no "back" to which to return.

Worlds of Philosophical Difference

Replacing Husserl's function of voice, in establishing the unity and origin of sense and presence, with a function of writing (which Husserl has repressed as exteriority), Derrida expresses himself as follows in raising the question of the identity of a signifying form: "Why is this identity paradoxically the division or dissociation of itself, which will make of this phonic sign a grapheme? Because this unity of the signifying form only constitutes itself by virtue of its iterability" ("Signature Event Context," p. 10). Are we thereby also meant to ask how we are to understand this tone, one which takes the paradox of identity—that two things can be the same thing, the morning star the same as the evening star, this occasion of the word "morning" to be of the same word as the following occurrence of the word "morning," this instance of a color to be the same color as that instance, this car to be the same as that, pain in this body to be the same pain as in that body, this person to be the same person he was—as a question of animism and pathos (of something's being "dissociated from itself")?

To respond to this question, or account for my response to it, I have to loop back to some passages in earlier work of mine.

In recasting Derrida's criticism of Husserl so as to mark the conjunction of phenomenological reduction with the method of doubt in sense-data (or sensibilia) theory, I have at the same time marked a connection between the section of my *Claim of Reason* that recites that conjunction ("Two Interpretations of Traditional Epistemology; Phenomenology") and the previous chapter of that book ("Excursus on Wittgenstein's Vision of Language"), a connection I had not seen before.

In a good sense the connection is not there apart from Husserl's metaphysical identification of the authority of voice and Derrida's criticism of it. The passages from *The Claim of Reason* are among its oldest, quite direct inclusions of my Ph.D. dissertation, submitted in 1961. The section on phenomenology and sense-data theory locates an adjacent, competing inquiry much in evidence around the Harvard philosophy department in the early 1950's, the years immediately preceding Austin's visiting semester. The inquiry was represented at Harvard in those years mainly, as the pertinent section of my doctoral dissertation ("Two Interpretations") records, by the work of my late colleague Roderick Firth, who played a significant role in the Saturday morning seminars, mentioned earlier, that Austin held on sense and sensibilia (and appearance and reality, and belief and knowledge, and certainty and empirical assertion, and presence and existence). (The section I included on this inquiry has little originality, but there is a considerable history to be recounted about its issues, of some pertinence to a number of distinguished American and English philosophers. Firth was a prominent student of C. I. Lewis, who retired from Harvard in 1953. Lewis's Kantian-inspired *Mind and the World Order* was one of the most academically influential philosophical books of the American 1930's, read, it happens, by Austin, who read few books of philosophy, and, I gather, read with interest by him but not cited among the philosophical texts he notes in *Sense and Sensibilia* as having "fallen for" the idea of a class of things such as sense-data. The immediate pertinence of this history to me is in part to remember the example of Lewis's seriousness and significance as a teacher of philosophy, and again to cite the importance to me of the work of Thompson Clarke, one of the last of Lewis's principal students at Harvard, who would go on to develop the legacy of classical epistemology with decisive originality.)

The other chapter I just cited from *The Claim of Reason*, on Wittgenstein's vision of language, however brief and swift, did seem to me to have a certain original way of looking at things, and now I find a, let's say, structural similarity between Derrida's criticism of Husserl's location of presence in the authority of the voice and mine of the classical empiricists' identification of the authority of the universal in thought as the generalization of a present idea, or word. My discussion in that chapter begins in effect with the quotation of a question from Locke's *Essay Concerning Human Understanding* (Book III, Chapter III): "Since all things that exist are only particulars, how come we by general terms [on which thinking depends]?" Cannot Husserl's question be framed analogously? Since language is only external, how does it come into the origin of self-presence [on which knowledge depends]? Though I did not, I might just possibly then, as now, have captured in my experience, and theorized, a fantasy of a voice that precedes language, that as it were gives itself language. This is not quite the fantasy of acquiring language by stealing it, since that carries the implication of coming late to language—not preceding it—so that there always remains a problem whether language is mine, something that giving myself language should precisely settle. (Unless, among other possibilities, I can, with Augustine, thank God for giving it to me.) In practice, however, the moment I felt that something about ordinary language philosophy was giving me a voice in philosophy, I knew that the something was the idea of a return of voice to philosophy, that asking myself what I say when, letting that matter, presented itself as a defiance of philosophy's interest in language, as if what philosophy meant by logic demanded, in the name of rationality, the repression of voice (hence of confession, hence of autobiography). Thus when in my second paper in philosophy, the first in response to reading Wittgenstein ("The Availability of Wittgenstein's Later Philosophy," placed as the introduction to my dissertation), I identified the *Investigations* as a form and work of confession, I set words out that I am following to this moment.

A summary of my response to Locke's picture of universality is given in the following paragraph from the chapter on Wittgenstein's vision of language (*Claim of Reason*, p. 188):

I think that what Wittgenstein ultimately wishes to show is that it *makes no sense* at all to give a general explanation for the generality of language, because it makes no sense at all to suppose words in general might *not* recur, that we might possess a name for a thing (say "chair" or "feeding") and yet be willing to call *nothing* (else) "the same thing." And even if you say, with Berkeley, that "an idea [or word] which considered in itself is particular, becomes general by being made to represent or stand for all other particular ideas of the same sort" *(Principles)*, Introduction) you still haven't explained *how* this word gets used for these various "particulars," nor what the significance is if it doesn't. This suggests that the effort to explain the generality of words is initiated by a prior step which produces the idea of a word as a "particular," a step of "considering it in itself." And what *is* that like? We learn words in *certain* contexts [not in all in which they may occur—what could this mean?] And after a while we are expected to know when and how the words are used in other contexts. This is obvious enough, and philosophers have always asked for an explanation of it. A famous answer is: Because there are universals. Locke and Berkeley are interpreting this request. Wittgenstein is dismantling it. [See *Claim of Reason*, p. 169.] What are we to take as the "particular" present here? Being willing to call other ideas (or objects) "the same sort" and being willing to use "the same word" for them is one and the same thing. The former does not explain the latter [or vice versa].

A way of putting the thought here is to say that the particularity of words does not consist in their material or spatial integrity; their criteria of identity are not the same as the criteria of identity of sticks and stones. This was an essential topic of a paper of mine a few years later ("Knowing and Acknowledging," begun in response to some work of Norman Malcolm's) on the subject of the knowledge of others, worked out to begin with touching on the concepts of colors and cars and pains, among other things. From that paper: "So here [in a case adapted from that of the Corsican Brothers] we have a pain [identified so as to distinguish it from other pains I might have] in *this* body and a pain in *that* body and it is numerically the same pain, literally the same. The thing which looked unintelligible, was so, only given a certain picture" (*Must We Mean What We Say?* p. 252). My ontological animus is, as it were, turned around in its original context, where I claim that having the same pain is as much like having the same car as it is like having the same color, so that one cannot be assured, as Malcolm wishes to be, that pains are just like colors, hence that there is just no question but that two people can have the same pain. In the case of the identity of words, where the type/token distinction applies, the aptness of the distinction makes it empty to ask which of two tokens of the same type is dissociated from the other, or which is, as it were, nearer or farther from their common type, which of them is in that way more original or purer. The chapter in question argues that it is empty to answer the question, "How do we know that 'feed the lion,' 'feed the meter,' and 'feed a person's pride' contain recurrences of the same word?" by replying, "They contain tokens of the same type." For Wittgenstein there can be no general explanation of this recurrence, or these (dis)continuations, for that would amount to an explanation of why language refers to the (or a) world and how it is that we share language; and either these questions are versions of Locke's question that takes the particularity of existence as the unquestionable thing, or they seek to avoid through metaphysics a recognition that there is no case in which the reference of a word or our sharing of it may not be contested.

Now take the question Derrida raises about the identity of a signifying form: "Why is this identity paradoxically the division or dissociation of itself, which will make of this phonic sign a grapheme? Because this unity of the signifying form only constitutes itself by virtue of its iterability." The idea in the second sentence, in terms of my response to Locke, and the follow-up response in thinking of others, would run: If the signifying form weren't recognized to recur, it wouldn't be a signifying form. It follows that "before" the recurrence (in writing) the occurrence (in sound, in the mouth), whatever particular it was, was not a signifying form. Where is the paradox?

An answer to be expected is that the particular becomes a universal in retrospect (*nachträglich*). But my problem remains over the "becomes." In introducing the animism of "division or dissociation of itself" into the idea of "recurrence" the picture is that the voice, the before, the inner, under its own power fissions into meaning. But this seems to give writing too little to do (awaiting the voice's approach), and too much (providing the linguistic as such). What's left out, as that chapter on Wittgenstein's vision of language goes on to explore, is that the iteration necessary for language comes from elsewhere—Wittgenstein pictures it rather as a continuation, or discrete continuability, knowing or seeing how to go on, but as if something is always over. The step creates the path as it relinquishes the path. The "recognition of recurrence," the form, comes from the place of the other, as it were from his or (surely) her resistance to and containing of the voice. On the second page of Wittgenstein's *Investigations,* in its second section, the builder is said to be issuing "calls" *(Rüfe)* to his assistant. This is evidently to indicate that we are not simply to assume that he is issuing (what we call) (full) words. Are we not thereby asked to wonder why words are (used in) calls? Does distance cause the call; or is it that the drive to call creates distance? Is this too obvious to mention?

But its implications, quite unobvious, significantly controversial, are emblematized in the passage of the *Investigations* that I call its scene of instruction and cited earlier: "If I have exhausted the justifications I have reached bedrock, and my spade is turned. Then I am inclined to say: 'This is simply what I do.'" Is it hard here to keep from a clash of wooden trivialities? The Wittgenstein quotation may be iterated as: If I've exhausted my cake I can't eat it; then I might fight you for some. Comparably Derrida: The signifying form repeats itself by virtue of its repeatability; or, differentiates itself by virtue of its differentiability.

Against the idea of a grapheme (I take it, a distinctive unit of writing)—as something essentially spaced, cut, separated, associated with death—Derrida's sense of the "paradoxicality" in this "unity" seems to insist on the pathos of the philosophical view of language that he combats, unless he is deliberately speaking in ironic indirect discourse and so mocks that pathos. There is too much of his writing I do not know for me to have confidence in my reaction. But how otherwise does the sense of paradox arise?—as if the orthodox thought of a "signifying form" is, again, what Locke expresses by assuming that "all things that exist are particulars." Is the pathos of writing allegorized by a literal distance—spacing—between inner intention and outer consequence, or by the distance between a word and its (transfigured) iteration, unknown to me, elsewhere? Are there such literal distances? There is such a distance between the sending and the receiving of a signal. There is no such distance between the saying of a word and the understanding or misunderstanding of the word, the one in my mind and the same one in yours. Closeness and remoteness there are not measured so. Then the pathos in the identity of my words is perhaps not that they exist beyond the control of my intention, in the fact that I do not understand all my words' arrivals (why should I? how could I?), but rather that I may be understood by them, in their return to me, too well. This suggests that the pathos is that of telepathy, mind-reading. I will want to distinguish this pathos of necessity of sense from what I will come to call the suffering of the necessity of action. The basis for such a distinction will take a while to appear.

Derrida's diagnosis of Husserl bears comparison with a favored form, in the other tradition, of the criticism of skepticism, as, for example, in a diagnosis by P. F. Strawson, a younger contemporary of Austin's at Oxford and an admired teacher of Searle's: "[The skeptic] pretends to accept a conceptual scheme, but at the same time quietly rejects one of the conditions of its employment" (quoted and commented on in *The Claim of Reason*, pp. 47–48). Austin brings something like this turn to Ayer's work, showing in effect that Ayer repudiates or represses the differences of that ordinary language on which his analysis depends. And Derrida will comparably ask of Austin's work on performatives: "For, ultimately, isn't it true that what Austin excludes as anomaly, exception, 'non-serious,' *citation* (on stage, in a poem, or a soliloquy) is the determined modification of a general citationality—or rather, a general iterability—without which there would not even be a 'success-ful' performative? So that—a paradoxical but unavoidable conclusion—a successful performative is necessarily an 'impure' performative, to adopt the word advanced later on by Austin when he acknowledges that there is no 'pure' performative." (I juxtapose here Derrida's "compara-ble" characterization of Husserl on signs: "Even while repressing differ-ence by assigning it to the exteriority of the signifiers, Husserl could not fail to recognize its work at the origin of sense and presence. Taking auto-affection as the exercise of the voice, auto-affection supposed that a pure difference comes to divide self-presence. In this pure difference is rooted the possibility of everything we think we can exclude from auto-affection: space, the outside, the world, the body, etc. As soon as it is admitted that auto-affection is the condition for self-presence, no pure transcendental reduction is possible" [*Speech and Phenomena*, p. 82]).

Having myself considered at some length in *The Claim of Reason* such a turn in philosophy's address to skepticism, I want to shift the texture of discussion here to a point at which I seem to hear the traditions scrape as they pass each other. For it seems to me that Austin's tone in philosophy, his mode of arrogation, is so opposed to Husserl's that no term of criticism that fits both is likely to be equally interesting philosophically about both—such as saying of Nietzsche and of Bertrand Russell that both are atheists. Put otherwise: Each side of the philosophical mind will have its reasons for finding the invitation to compare Husserl and Ayer ludicrous, but it might be worth hearing what the reasons are. Each might judge the comparison to be imperti-nent. To what? Well, to the importance of the tradition that has led to the present of the one making the judgment. (Directions of interest that were separate in *The Claim of Reason* now seem to have become inextricable. In roughly the first three parts of that book, "tradition" in philosophy means old against new, where new mostly means what comes [historically] with the analytical revolution[s]; in the fourth part, "tradition" comes to mark the rift of one [cultural] tradition against another, each of which splits into its old and its new.)

Pictures of Destruction

Different traditions will propose different views of pertinence and importance. A remark from Wittgenstein's *Investigations* may come to mind: "Where does our investigation get its importance from, since it seems only to destroy everything interesting; that is, all that is great and important? (As it were all the buildings, leaving behind only bits of stone and rubble.) What we are destroying is nothing but houses of cards and we are clearing up the ground of language on which they stand" (§ 118). I believe some attentive readers of Wittgenstein have taken this passage to deny that he is destroying anything, hence to leave unanswered the question where "our" investigation gets its importance from. Of course there is that clause about clearing up language, but *that* accomplishment does not distinguish Wittgenstein from, say, logical positivism, and Wittgenstein (the later especially) would suffer from the comparison, since from that perspective he seems as mired in the vagueness, imprecision, and inexactness of everyday language as all philosophy chronically appears to have been, in the eyes of the analytical revolutions (but in which philosophical eyes not?). Still, in a sense the reading of the passage as failing to answer the question of importance is correct, as correct as a reading of it to extract a certain form of answer. What it says is that our investigation gets its importance from what it destroys, and in particular from its destruction of a construction of fantasy, precisely a fantasy of importance. The parenthetical sentence between Wittgenstein's question and his response is some initial articulation of the fantasy, as one of destruction ("As it were all the buildings, leaving behind only bits of stone and rubble"). Is this articulation perhaps arbitrary, or some unnamed effort to lend color to an abstract conceptual moment? Could its color have been evoked as the destruction of a forest by logging equipment, or of a field of flowers by the gathering for a summer concert or by the march of an army? Not, I think, if the idea is that we are going to have to pick up the pieces and find out how and whether to go on, that is, go on living in this very place of devastation, as of something over.

Something of the sort is, it seems to me, at stake when Derrida, in the last sentence of the excerpt I cut from his concluding pages of *Speech and Phenomena*, finds that what "begins" "beyond" the closure of the history of being as presence will require "un-heard of thoughts. . . , sought for across the memory of old signs." I respond to this also as a fantasy of destruction, or of deconstruction—not perhaps so much one of having been attacked as one of decay or ruin. But in any case, while there is no question of responsibility for the fact of this crossroads, or the lost roads, of human history, there is a declaration of participation in a scene of aftermath, a calling for a task of some kind, as if *this*, our present circumstances, cannot stand—if only a calling for the task of calling, that is, for an assembling of a reconceived remembering. How change is to come is accordingly of the greatest moment.

I note briefly two earlier fantasies of intellectual destruction that may be playing a role in those I have just cited and are produced by voices already called upon in these pages. The first is from *Thus Spoke Zarathustra:* "I walk among the fragments and limbs of men. This is what is terrible for my eyes, that I find man in ruins and scattered as over a battlefield or a butcher-field." That is the last sentence of an excerpt from *Zarathustra* identified previously as the epigraph used by Derrida for his discussion, in *Otobiographies*, of Nietzsche's *Ecce Homo*. I cited the first sentence of the epigraph, on "inverse cripple[s] who have too little of everything and too much of one thing"—a big eye or a big mouth or a big belly or a big ear—and claimed it was Nietzsche's transcription of a passage from Emerson's "The American Scholar" on "walking monsters."

The end of the passage used by Derrida is also, as it happens, a transcription of an Emerson sentence, also from "The American Scholar," which is accordingly the second of the earlier passages of destruction I have paused to adduce: "This revolution [in human aspiration] is to be wrought by the gradual domestication of the idea of Culture. The main enterprise of the world for splendor, for extent, is the upbuilding of a man. Here are materials strewn along the ground." The destruction in Emerson's passage is, as one would expect, easier to sense in Nietzsche's transcription of it; but it was clear enough when I quoted it to somewhat different effect (emphasizing upbuilding and Culture) a few years ago in *This New Yet Unapproachable America*. While I do not assume Derrida had recognized the Emersonian origins in Nietzsche's passages, neither am I prepared to take the coincidence lightly; I am prepared to pose a consistency of ear that ought to inspire and sustain some accounting.

Derrida's Austin and the Stake of Positivism

The ear's returning is a cue, in my turning now somewhat more consecutively to Derrida's encounter with Austin in "Signature Event Context," to go back to my remark about Austin's difference of tone and ask why Derrida is not, perhaps cannot be, further interested in its difference from that of the other philosophers whose margins he covers. In Paris that summer I twice asked Derrida questions specifically motivated by directions my work was taking that I was unprepared for—questions I had no reason to believe my contemporaries in philosophy at home would be interested in—concerning what I had in the title essay of *Must We Mean What We Say?* called the sound of philosophy. I had subtitled that book *A Book of Essays* to register a problem about what a book of philosophy is, or, I sometimes said, should look like—given that the idea of what a philosophy article is, and should be, was well established and monitored professionally in the Anglo-American context (it is a scientific or scholarly text, the proof of disciplinary competence, and as such the basis of academic appointment and promotion, and so on), and given that the two longest essays in that first book of mine (on *Endgame* and on *Lear*) obviously did not fit that idea, and that much of the tone of the rest of the book was, for richer or poorer, rather over the edge. I had had fancies of putting that book out in a newspaper format, so that each essay could begin on the front page and end on the back page, with various conjunctions in between. Fortunately or not, given American publishing then, and my lack of say in such matters, nothing came of this.

It was on my mind when I asked Derrida, innocently, what he imagined a page of philosophy might otherwise look like—a question that received (so I took it) a prolonged silence, which I took kindly. Some years later, on opening Derrida's *Glas*, I was embarrassed in retrospect (hardly for the first time) by my innocence. When I asked that question I was contemplating a little book on *Walden* and I had been asking myself specifically how Thoreau's philosophical purposes were served—and disguised—by cultivating the sound of a moralizing, autobiographical historian of nature. This was on my mind when on another morning, after a demonstration by Derrida of his mode of reading, taking as his text a sonnet of Mallarmé's ("Or") I asked why, accepting the brilliance of the demonstration, the Mallarmé text is so careful to preserve its look. Again there was silence, which again I took kindly, but nothing has happened since to embarrass the question, and I find I want, in that spirit, to ask Derrida—I mean his text—what he takes Austin's tone to be, why his writing looks as it does. (Well, like academic lectures; but so does Heidegger's *What Is Called Thinking?* significantly take the form of academic lectures. Austin and Heidegger might even both be said to resist the form. This makes them all the more different from each other.)

Austin's tone is a pertinent question for "Signature Event Context," since Derrida there pays Austin an unusually handsome string of compliments, calling his analysis of performative utterances "patient, open, aporetical, in constant transformation, often more fruitful in the acknowledgment of its impasses than its positions" (p. 14). These precious predicates are doubtless awarded out of a recognition of specific further affinities of Derrida's work with Austin's—both are philosophers of limitation, both interested in the morality and politics of speech (out of something like a shared sense that concepts, without the most scrupulous attention, impose, and are imposed, upon us), and both take the struggle against metaphysics as a struggle for liberation, for something more than reason, as it were, itself. Most significantly, perhaps, there is an appreciation of the fact that Austin's analysis of the performative may be seen to be motivated precisely as an attack on what deconstruction attacks under the name logocentricism.

I take logocentrism—I speak hesitantly and use phrases from *Speech and Phenomena*—to name a "limitation of sense to knowledge, of logos to objectivity, of language to reason" (p. 99), amounting to "the unity of thought and voice in logos" (p. 74), from which Husserl had at once started and stopped an effort at "the emancipation of speech as nonknowing" (p. 97). (I once put what I gather to be a congenial thought by formulating an intuition I find shared by thinkers from Emerson to Wittgenstein to the effect that our fundamental relation to the world is not one of knowing.) Austin refers to this limitation as "the descriptive fallacy," though he objects to the name, and describes the fallacy in the opening sentence of the second paragraph of *How to Do Things With Words*, as follows: "It was for too long the assumption of philosophers that the business of a 'statement' can only be to 'describe' some state of affairs, or to 'state some fact,' which it must do either truly or falsely."

Austin's so-called theory of speech acts is in effect the presentation of a massive set of (sets of) counter-examples to this assumption (a set that proves to have interests well beyond this initial interest), which is to say, examples in which what are grammatically statements are *not* in the business of stating facts truly or falsely. Opening instances of such counter-examples are: "I do," "I name this ship the *Queen Elizabeth*," "I give and bequeath my watch to my brother," "I bet you a dollar it will rain tommorrow." Austin comments: "In these examples it seems

clear that to utter the sentence (in, of course, the appropriate circumstances) is not to *describe* my doing of what I should be said in so
uttering to be doing, or to state that I am doing it: it is to do it. None
of the utterances cited is either true or false: I assert this as obvious
and do not argue it" (pp. 5, 6).

By the deflationary phrase "not the business of a 'statement'" Austin
comes as close as he can to saying, in Derrida's terms, not "[the]
internal and positive condition of possibility [of language]" ("Signature
Event Context," p. 17). Derrida was bound to be drawn to Austin's
discoveries. But when he says that "Austin was obliged to free the
analysis of the performative from the authority of the truth *value . . .*
and to substitute for it at times the value of force, of difference of force
(*illocutionary* or *perlocutionary force*) . . . which is nothing less than
Nietzschean" (p. 13), I find that Derrida's sense of the matter is something like the reverse of mine.

Austin's introduction of an idea of force, his "substitution" of something about force for something about truth is meant not as a revelation
of truth as illusion or as will to power (if something of the sort is what
Derrida signals as "Nietzschean"), but rather as specifying the extent to
which what may be called the value of truth—call it an adequation of
language and reality, or a discovering of reality—is on the contrary as
essential to performative as to constative utterances. To this extent an
aporia in the way of distinguishing between performatives and constatives is as much to Austin's philosophical liking as it is to his classifica-
tory dismay.

Austin's insistence on the (value of) adequation between performatives and reality (the various empirical, factual conditions whose satisfaction constitutes an utterance as the performative it is) positions his
argumentative move as, whatever else, a specific and (then) current
counter to logical positivism, specifically to positivism's notorious claim
that utterances other than statements are lacking in a measure of
rationality, or, say, adequation to reality. Such utterances—for example,
judgments of aesthetics, of ethics, and of religion—were held by these

philosophers to contain a brand of meaning inferior to that enjoyed by verifiable statements, namely, so-called emotive meaning as opposed to cognitive or scientific meaning, and were held therefore as unamenable to (further) philosophical assessment. When Derrida interprets Austin as "[substituting] . . . at times the value of force for the value of truth," this directly negates, destroys, Austin's counter to positivism, which depends upon an understanding of the performative utterance as *retaining* an adequation to reality (to certain factual conditions) equal to that of verifiable statements. Which is a way of saying that Austin's work in the theory of performatives is designed precisely to retain "the value of truth."

What Austin "substitutes" for the logically defined concept of truth is *not force but "felicity."* Statements, if adequate to reality, are true, if not, false. (This defines the concept of a statement.) Performatives, if adequate to reality, are felicitous, if not, then, in specific ways, infelicitous.

The idea of "[substituting] at times the value of force for the authority of the truth value" might be taken as an interpretation of positivism's understanding of meaning, in the following way. "Force," for Austin, comes up when, elaborating his theory, he comes to distinguish two kinds of what might be called performatives, two kinds of utterances which are meaningful but do not state facts: utterances that do something *in* saying something and utterances that do something *by* saying something, a difference registered in Austin's naming the former illocutionary utterances, the latter perlocutionary. Examples of the illocutionary are the cases, by now familiar, of betting, bequeathing, warning, promising, and so on. Examples of the perlocutionary are persuading, annoying, thrilling, bullying, frightening, wounding, and so on. Illocutionary utterances take over and further articulate the cases Austin began by simply calling performatives (as opposed to constatives). Perlocutionary utterances can be seen to locate, even to corner, the characteristic cases of positivism's emotive utterances (as opposed to cognitive utterances); but it does not come into Austin's enterprise,

as it was left, and perhaps meant to be left, to articulate the perlocutionary much further.

A grammatical touchstone of illocutionary force is that the utterance
can regularly be introduced in the first-person singular present indicative active ("I bet you," "I give and bequeath to my brother"), whereas
the perlocutionary cannot, except by accident, so be introduced. To say
"I persuade (annoy, arouse, wound) you" is not, except perhaps by
Gothic arrangement, to persuade, arouse, wound you—though such
utterances may form an introduction to some acknowledgment of how
I undertake, or have undertaken, to do such things. Now since there is
no reason to believe that Austin for some reason fails to regard annoying or wounding someone, or persuading them of something, as something language is as fully capable of conveying as it is of conveying bets
and gifts, it follows that the presence of the first-person singular pro-
noun in illocutionary utterance marks a local feature of such convey-
ance, not a global opportunity for Austin to define communication—
not even as a missed "ideal"—as essentially a function of "the presence
to self of a total context, the transparence of intentions, the presence
of meaning to the absolutely singular uniqueness of a speech act, etc."
("Signature Event Context," p. 17). Positivism's stake, accordingly, may
be said to lie in a picture of non-cognitive (preeminently, non-scien-
tific) utterances as containing force *as a substitute for meaning*. And to
oppose this scientistically enforced picture of a uniform brand (or two
such brands) of "meaning" is as deep and pervasive a part of Austin's
rigor, patience, and so forth, as to dislodge truth from its philosophically imperialist adventures. They are indeed parts of the same project.
There is a Nietzschean drift in Austin's views, but in another direction,
which I will later try to plot.

It is not possible here, briefly, to re-create the climate in which
positivism was pervasive and dominant in the Anglo-American academic world, from the mid-1940's through the 1950's and beyond,
almost throughout the humanities and the social sciences—a hege-
monic presence more total, I believe, than that of any one of today's

politically or intellectually advanced positions. Positivism during this period was virtually unopposed on any intellectually organized scale. And no publication was more successful in popularizing logical positivism—no work of academic philosophy was itself more popular, or more cited and required in philosophy courses—than A. J. Ayer's *Language, Truth, and Logic*. Austin's violence toward Ayer's *Foundations of Empirical Knowledge* was evidently in long preparation.

I do not suppose Derrida recognizes (or would attach decisive importance to) Austin's argumentative appointment with positivism, yet it seems to me that he may be an unusual beneficiary of it, not only of Austin's score against it but also of positivism's own continuing powers (altered, not vanquished, by the failings of its stake in a general program of reducing, or elevating, philosophy to the image of logic). I mean that the positivist sensibility will have helped prepare deconstruction's occupation of literary (and social) studies comparably to the way pragmatism helped prepare logical positivism's occupation of departments of philosophy in America three decades earlier. Above all, understandably I trust, I cite deconstruction's and positivism's comparable flights from the ordinary, however different their ways and means.

And I cite their claims to what may be seen as the discovery of the originariness of writing over voice, of system over individual intervention, of sign over word—since the appeal to mathematical logic for its algorithmic value is an appeal to its sublime inscriptional powers (of alignment, rewriting, iteration, substitution, and so on). Positivism's inscriptionality may be seen as in service of a homogenization of the field of sense, and so ought to appear to deconstruction as the last word in, or a surrealist reversal of, (deconstruction's view of) philosophy's view of writing as (merely, or sheerly) extending a homogenously conceived semantic field of the voice: the last, or surrealist, word since writing proves to have its own homogeneity, further occluding room for deconstruction's interpretation of that differentiation (via inscription) on which signification depends. (Unless Gödel's proofs are to be metaphorized as the provision of a limit to homogeneity. I should perhaps say—though the issue of the relation of voice and writing will keep coming up—that the idea of such a metaphorization strikes me as an effort to invite the strength of mathematics and the strength of ordinary language to destroy each other. For what gain?) At the same time, positivism's proposal of a derivative, homogenous field of the emotivity of language (containing whatever is expressed by grammatical statements that are neither empirically verifiable nor logically provable) is congenial with Derrida's projection of what from Austin's perspective seems a homogenous field of the performativity of language (producing "effects").

(An inner connection between positivism and other formations of "Continental philosophy" has made itself felt in my work from its first years, a major cause of my, let's say, ambivalence toward deconstruction. I quote from *Must We Mean What We Say?* "While Kierkegaard's account . . . sometimes seems to rebuke us for being confused about a meaning which should be clear with a qualitatively decisive clarity, . . . he would nevertheless not be surprised at positivism's claim, or perception, that religious utterances have *no* cognitive meaning. Indeed, he might welcome this fact. It indicates that the crisis of our age has deepened, that we are no longer *confused*, and that we have a chance, at last, to learn what our lives really depend upon. Utterances we have shared about our infinite interests no longer carry any cognitive meaning. Well and good; we have now completely forgotten it. Then it is up to each of us to find our own" ["Kierkegaard's *On Authority and Revelation*," pp. 171–172]. This is to be compared with the hearsay accusation against deconstruction to the effect that it holds language to be meaningless, a helpless jab that deconstructionists of my acquaintance have relished the ease of mocking, while none to my knowledge has articulated its source. Perhaps it is not that hard. Yet the illusoriness in the charge seems to me assayable, if I may say so, in the light of another essay in that first book of mine: "Positivism said that statements about God are meaningless; Beckett shows that they mean too damned much"

["Ending the Waiting Game," p. 120]. Positivism possesses as much claim to have become itself in America as deconstruction does.)

Since the adequation to reality Austin wishes to preserve in non-descriptive or non-constative utterances is not metaphysical adequation, his analysis has to recognize that "failure is an essential risk of the operations under consideration" (see "Signature Event Context," p. 15), which might be glossed as the claim that truth in human terms everywhere suffers inadequation, that our words are always outrun by the real, or, as Derrida puts it in one of the flights of the last pages of *Speech and Phenomena*, "The thing itself always escapes." Yet Derrida takes Austin to deny this, or rather, in the words I just now cited of Derrida's, takes Austin to deny—instead of, as I take Austin, to affirm in every sentence, in each of his characteristic methodological jokes or mottoes—that "failure is an essential risk of the operations under consideration," which I understand to say that if utterances *could* not fail they would not be the human actions under consideration, indeed not the actions of humans at all. Why does Derrida think otherwise of Austin?

Part of an answer lies in the way Derrida reads what he calls Austin's rejecting, deferring, and excluding (see "Signature Event Context," p. 16) of a "'general theory'" (ibid.) that would "[interrogate] as an essential predicate or as a *law* . . . the value of risk or exposure to infelicity" (ibid., p. 15) in all acts and utterances. Derrida goes on to cite two exclusions, in the first of which Austin says:

> Now I suppose some very general high-level doctrine might embrace both what we have called infelicities *and* these other "unhappy" features of the doing of actions. . . . We must just remember, though, that features of this [latter] sort can and do constantly obtrude into any case we are discussing. Features of this sort would normally come under the heading of "extenuating circumstances" or of "factors reducing or abrogating the agent's responsibility," and so on.

I note that Austin's assertion that "features of this sort can and *do constantly* obtrude" (my emphasis) does not sound to me as if he is excluding these features from awareness and significance. But this does not satisfy Derrida: "Austin does not ponder the consequences issuing from the fact that a possibility—a possible risk—is *always* possible, and is in some sense a necessary possibility. Nor whether—once such a necessary possibility of infelicity is recognized—infelicity still constitutes an accident" (*ibid.* p. 15). "Not ponder the consequences" evidently asks for a different level of discussion, one that gives an account of, or "interrogates as an essential predicate or *law*," these constantly obtruding features described by Austin.

Exclusion of the Theory of Excuses: On the Tragic

It is hard to conceive that one who has read through Austin's comparatively small quantity of writing will fail to recognize that the headings Austin suggests for what the doctrine he has just excluded is a doctrine or theory of—"extenuating circumstances" and "factors reducing or abrogating the agent's responsibility" (which Austin places in quotation marks as indicating, I assume, that he is quoting something he takes as well enough known to need no more than reminding of)—are headings that refer to Austin's own work on excuses, summarized, as said earlier, in one of his thirteen collected papers. It is the paper of Austin's that is marked, moreover, by containing his most extended broaching (consisting of all of eight pages) of the even more general theory concerning his philosophical methods of attending to ordinary language. I accordingly conclude that Austin has excluded this general doctrine only from explicit discussion in *How to Do Things with Words* ("I am not going into the general doctrine here"), that in saying so he is implicitly including it, in his way, in asking us to "remember" its pertinence. (It perhaps describes this situation to say that Derrida iterated Austin's views without knowing this piece of them. So what? It happens. But isn't something of the kind to be said about Searle's iteration of Derrida's views? What was surprising, given Searle's context, in his account? I hope I am not confounding the iteration that makes language possible with the iteration that makes scholarship possible. An ordinary language analysis of communication should have something to say about this.)

Excuses are as essentially implicated in Austin's view of human actions as slips and over-determination are in Freud's. What does it betoken about human actions that the reticulated constellation of predicates of excuse is made for them—that they can be done unintentionally, unwillingly, involuntarily, insincerely, unthinkingly, inadvertently, heedlessly, carelessly, under duress, under the influence, out of contempt, out of pity, by mistake, by accident, and so on? (To experience Austin's meticulous journey through his world of concrete examples of these qualifications—and scores of others—is for the moment to put aside all question of how we know such things, or whether to know them is philosophy.) It betokens, we might say, the all but unending vulnerability of human action, its openness to the independence of the world and the preoccupation of the mind. I would like to say that the theme of excuses turns philosophy's attention patiently and thoroughly to something philosophy would love to ignore—the fact that human life is constrained to the life of the human body, to what Emerson calls the giant I always take with me. The law of the body is the law.

Who, such as Austin, would so dwell on excuses who did not surmise that the human necessity for action, and of action for motion, is apt to become unbearable—its consequences, concomitants, upshots, effects, results, and so forth (another favorite chain of Austin's) unsurveyable, the body a parchment of its displacements. (Who but one familiar with despair would so insist on taking joy—like Emerson and after him Nietzsche?) Excuses mark out the region of tragedy, the beyond of the excusable, the justifiable, the explainable (the civil?). Who among philosophers has a theory of forgiveness, and whether it is givable? It would be a theory of comedy.

This route to the sense of the unbearableness of human action—of its over-determination and its over-indebtedness, as of the unreachableness of justice—is a kind of interpretation of Nietzsche's perception of what, in section 7 of *The Birth of Tragedy* he sees as Hamlet's lethargy, experienced with nausea. This is the point at which I predicted a Nietzschean element will come into Austin's work. It is the most sensitive point of Austin's inscription of tragedy—say, of the tragic hedge of ordinary life—in his invocation of Euripides' *Hippolytus* in the opening lecture of *How to Do Things with Words*. This point is rather disguised in Austin's comments on Hippolytus, and I did not for a long time understand the inscription with sufficient seriousness.

Austin at that moment is combating his mortal philosophical enemy, or one of its recurring faces, the craving for profundity. (This characterisically goes in Austin with a questioning of philosophy's intellectual seriousness. But the other faces of philosophy's enemy are marked in nothing short of the endless list of his terms of criticism of other philosophy.) The question of profundity arises here in Austin's deflecting of a charge against his view that it is superficial or, as he puts the charge here, "flippant." The charge is that his view, according to which saying something is sometimes doing something, really just comes to claiming that "to marry is to say a few words" or "betting is simply saying something" (p. 7). Austin goes on to try lessening the sound of flippancy by emphasizing the importance of specific circumstances in the uttering of performatives, but soon his diagnosis of the sense of his superficiality darkens.

Exclusion of the Theory of the Non-Serious

I quote most of two paragraphs, both to suggest how immeasurably complex the issues are that I am tracking here in a few strokes, and to mark that on the pivot of profundity I have turned to the second of the two general doctrines Derrida charges Austin with excluding from his discussion of performatives. The first, the doctrine of excuses, to repeat, takes up the failures performatives share with all actions; the second is the doctrine that takes up the failure performatives share with all utterances.

> But we may, in objecting [on the ground of apparent superficiality in the suggestion that doing something is merely a matter of saying some words], have something totally different, and this time quite mistaken, in mind, especially when we think of some of the more awe-inspiring performatives such as "I promise to . . ." Surely the words must be spoken "seriously" and so as to be taken "seriously"? This is, though vague, true enough in general—it is an important commonplace in discussing the purport of any utterance whatsoever. I must not be joking, for example, nor writing a poem. But we are apt to have a feeling that their being serious consists in their being uttered as (merely) the outward and visible sign, for convenience or other record or for information, of an inward and spiritual act: from which it is but a short step to go on to believe or to assume without realizing that for many purposes the outward utterance is a description, *true or false,* of the occurrence of the inward performance. The classic expression of this idea is to be found in the *Hippolytus* (l. 612), where Hippolytus says . . . "My tongue swore to, but my heart [or mind or other backstage artiste—Austin's addition] did not." Thus "I promise to . . ." obliges me—puts on record my spiritual assumption of a spiritual shackle.
>
> It is gratifying to observe in this very example how excess of profundity, or rather solemnity, at once paves the way for immorality. For one who says "Promising is not merely a matter of uttering words. It is an inward and spiritual act" is apt to appear as a solid moralist standing out against a generation of superficial theorizers: we see him as he sees himself, surveying the invisible depths of ethical space, with all the distinction of a specialist in the *sui generis.* Yet he provides Hippolytus with a let-out, the bigamist with an excuse for his "I do" and the welsher with a defence for his "I bet." Accuracy and morality alike are on the side of the plain saying that *our word is our bond.*
> (pp. 9–10)

When Austin later "excludes" this sort of material from (further) discussion, he flags it hurriedly, in the passage Derrida cites:

> Secondly, as *utterances* [versus as actions] our performances are *also* heir to certain other kinds of ill, which infect *all* utterances. And these

likewise, though again they might be brought into a more general account, we are deliberately at present excluding. I mean, for example, the following: a performative utterance will, for example, be *in a peculiar way* hollow or void if said by an actor on the stage, or if introduced in a poem, or spoken in soliloquy. This applies in a similar manner to any and every utterance—a sea-change in special circumstances. Language in such circumstances is in special ways—intelligibly—used not *seriously* [my emphasis, J.D.], but in many ways *parasitic* upon its normal use—ways which fall under the doctrine of the *etiolations* of language. All this we are *excluding* from consideration. Our performative utterances, felicitous or not, are to be understood as issued in ordinary circumstances. ("Signature Event Context," p. 16)

(When Hippolytus says, "My tongue swore to, but my heart did not," is he an actor on a stage? Does he think he is, that is, take himself to be on some inner stage? Does Austin imagine one or other of these possibilities to be in effect? Does Austin think we, or anyone at any time, may not be able to tell these differences? Or not tell them in the case of Hyppolytus because we cannot tell them in ourselves? Is there something in the figure of Hippolytus that would confuse Austin about all this? His slam at the "backstage artiste" suggests that there is. I am trying not to let such questions take over.) Derrida introduces this block of quotation in the following way:

The second case of this exclusion concerns our subject more directly. It involves precisely the possibility for every. . . . utterance . . . to be "quoted." . . . [Austin] insists on the fact that this possibility remains *abnormal, parasitic,* that it constitutes a kind of extenuation or agonized succumbing of language that we should strenuously distance ourselves from and ignore. And the concept of the "ordinary," thus of "ordinary language," to which he has recourse is clearly marked by this exclusion.

Derrida's saying "the second case of this exclusion" and, after the quotation, his speaking of "the whole general theory" seem clearly to take Austin to be excluding one theory twice rather than invoking two separate theories; and again he does not take Austin's qualification "at present" as registering that he has elsewhere developed, or begun developing, the theory in question.

But what the doctrine of excuses does for cases of extenuation, Austin's work represented in his paper "Pretending" (first published in 1958) in part does for, and is meant eventually to do more for, cases of etiolation, parasitism, and in general the realm of the "non-serious"; it is the place in which pretending is linked with, and initially defined so as to be distinguishable from, feigning or posing as, affecting or shamming, mimicking or merely imitating, rehearsing or acting (see "Pretending," p. 267). I suggested that Austin was not satisfied with this beginning; I recall his saying that he had been led to publish it prematurely. (That is itself a vignette that speaks to differences between the traditions of philosophy in their theories and institutions of publishing. I do not imagine French intellectuals pained at having published prematurely. Born into French publishing life, they print what a given time calls for. That would have, *mutatis mutandi,* its own attractions for Austin's sense of, even yearning for, the provisional.)

But should Austin's "Pretending" make matters better or worse with respect to Derrida's sense of something essential under exclusion? Is Austin creating exiles and then classifying them? Or is he rather verifying membership by charting its unruliness? He is surely denying that a necessity of misrule is claimable as a private exemption from rules. And he is surely denying that language (culture, the human life form) could exist in the absence of a difference between rule and misrule, which is to say, in the absence of difference. (I do not think I invent in remembering Austin's once observing, with poorly concealed mirth, "It couldn't *all* be horses!") I note for future reference my claim, in *The Claim of Reason,* that it is the difference between Austinian criterial differences (for example, between goldfinches and goldcrests) and Wittgensteinian non-criterial differences (for example, between rain and the appearance of rain) that makes skepticism possible. The differences among excuses are criterial; the differences between imitation, pretending, and so on, and what they imitate or pretend (to be real, to be sincere, and so on) are non-criterial. Austin in practice is sensitive to this meta-difference but in theory he makes no room for the non-criterial (at one point in "Other Minds" he insists, as if it is incontestably true, that since we know the difference between sleeping and waking there must be criteria that tell us the difference), which means to me that for Austin skepticism *cannot* be a serious intellectual quandary.

I doubt that anyone who cares about Austin's work would think "Pretending" to be the equal, in originality or in fecundity, of "A Plea for Excuses," so I will just quote the characteristic concluding paragraph of "Pretending" to secure the idea of the kind of work I am saying Austin meant it to do:

> What, finally, is the importance of all this about pretending? I will answer this shortly, although I am not sure importance is important: truth is. In the first place, it does seem that philosophers, who are fond of invoking pretending, have exaggerated its scope and distorted its meaning. In the second place, in the long-term project of classifying and clarifying all possible ways and varieties of *not exactly doing things*, which has to be carried through if we are ever to understand properly what doing things is, the clarification of pretending, and the assignment to it of its proper place within the family of related concepts, must find some place, if only a humble one.

If we do not at once take up the phantasm in this passage of assigning proper places in a family, we might let it make us consider again what the force is of Austin's excluding something from his analysis of (performative) language.

I should say that I do not imagine such a doctrine of pretending, however corrected and extended, doing for cases of the non-serious what excuses do for cases of extenuation. To glimpse why, I ask, comparably to the question I asked about the theory of excuses, what it betokens about utterance or about action that they can suffer, say, imitation (to take that title for the iterative). It betokens, roughly, that human utterances are essentially vulnerable to insincerity and that the realization that we may never know whether others are sincere (I do not exclude the first person) is apt to become unbearable. (We might say that it returns philosophy's attention to the fact that human life is constrained to the life of the mind, such as it is.) The reason for my lack of confidence in Austin's theory of pretending eventually to uncover such matters is that the family of concepts associated with it is one that contrasts with the knowledge or the reality or genuineness of action as a whole, a contrast that arises in skepticism with respect to minds at the place that the possibilities of dreaming and hallucination and illusion arise in skepticism with respect to things; and Austin's survey of that site is compatible with the view, or enforces it, that philosophical skepticism cannot be a serious intellectual stance.

This is too critical a point either merely to touch on or sensibly to take up here. It may help if I simply try to come at it briefly another way.

I am taking it that Austin's work in "Pretending" is not a serious interpretation of Austin's doubts about seriousness. There will be further interpretations Austin ventures of philosophy's unseriousness about the serious, other false profundities he will seek to expose (religious and political, as well as philosophical)—still one of his most unfashionable philosophical traits. Then why, given his impatience with philosophy as it stands, does he not simply or just ignore this particular failing of philosophy (its apparent need to be warned not to joke or soliloquize or poetize more or less at random)? Surely the detail of Austin's attacks on, among other matters, descriptivism or, we might name it, assertionism (if not logocentrism) is successful without that? But there is, I suggest, an as it were professional reason that he cannot just ignore it, a reason that he is forced to consider the issue of theater, jokes, and so forth, as if for a moment it were a threat to his theory of language, whereas he regards it—or should be expected to regard it—as a further part of his various investigations of doing (or saying) and of not quite doing (or saying) something. That a human performance may be humanly imitated (on a stage or in the street) pertains to his analysis of the performative in whatever way the fact that there are decoys or paintings of birds pertains to his analysis of the basis of knowing and naming birds, stuffed in a cage or real in a gutter.

I argue in Part One of *The Claim of Reason* that Austin's way of uncovering the issue of reality as a separate, "further" step (beyond naming) in assessing claims to know the world, and others and oneself in it (well, "others," "in," "it"), marks a key step in articulating the drive of skepticism. The difference of "level" (metaphysical? conceptual? logical?) between identifying the bird as a goldfinch *rather than* a goldcrest, and accepting this goldfinch as real, *that is to say, in this case,* not stuffed or a toy, is, if I may say so, a real difference, a fateful one. In my discussion in *The Claim of Reason,* I note something like this difference as one between what Wittgenstein sees as our telling things from one another by means of criteria we find we have fixed for ourselves and our non-criterial assumption of the shifts between reality and dreams, fantasies, poetry, painting, theater—shifts classically studied in part under the title of "imitation," and noted in passing in the passages featured prominently in Derrida's citations from *How to Do Things with Words* as the action or reaction of a "sea-change" in language. Now suppose that epistemological skepticism was not taken fully seriously in professional philosophy as a standing threat, after Kant's settlement with it, until Wittgenstein's *Investigations.* (I am speaking of this stretch of history as one leading back from Austin; hence I am not considering the guises skepticism may be taking in, say, Hegel and Nietzsche and Heidegger.) It nevertheless, or accordingly, may be seen to manifest itself as a kind of occupational hazard, in a philosopher's affecting cautions like "But how do you know you weren't hallucinating, or under the effects of a drug, or that the person wasn't feigning or acting a part, perhaps as a joke . . .?"

Since Austin did not, in some significant sense could not, take the step of imagining the conditions of skepticism to be, or to have been, a comprehensible drive, harboring perhaps, perhaps covering, certain extreme forms of human seriousness, he encountered it mostly in its passing (flippant?) manifestations. These then caused him to bristle rather than to consider; and then, with a show of collegiality, to hide the bristle. When the issue of seriousness is initially opened by Austin in that same passage from the first chapter of *How to Do Things with Words* which produces Hippolytus, he frames it as one of those semi-questions that indicate they are asserting a proposition too obvious to quite say: "Surely the words must be spoken 'seriously' and so as to be taken 'seriously?'" He goes on to concede what goes without more than semi-saying: "This is, though vague, true enough in general—it is an important commonplace in discussing the purport of any utterance whatsoever. I must not be joking, for example, nor writing a poem," nor be, it occurs to him to state in the next chapter, an actor on the stage. I note the designation "commonplace in discussing." What he is about to take up is not a simple or sheer commonplace, one you might come across in common places. For what, in such places, would we be urging upon one another commonly in proposing that we speak so as to be taken "seriously"? Good advice might be not to speak while chewing gum or while wearing a comic hat or while in an uncontrollable fit of winking (all pertinent, if well-worn, gags, doubtless born of the same anxieties as these solemner discussions of doubts about being taken seriously). What is an important commonplace *in discussing* is evidently a commonplace in philosophical discussion, and this is not the raising simply of the question of the seriousness of discussion but of the interpretation of seriousness as the contrast with joking, for example, or writing a poem, or soliloquizing on a stage.

What is the provenance of this "commonplace" "interpretation"? A plausible candidate is the epochal work of Frege (one of whose major texts was translated by Austin) in establishing modern logic. The classical source here is "On Sense and Reference," from 1892; but the issue is more slowly spelled out in "Logic" (the first of two essays with that title), in Frege's *Posthumous Writings*, for example at p. 130:

> If the sense of an assertoric sentence is not true, it is either false or fictitious, and it will generally be the latter if it contains a mock proper name. The writer, in common with, for example, the painter, has his

eye on appearances. Assertions in fiction are not to be taken seriously: they are only mock assertions. Even the thoughts are not to be taken seriously, as in the sciences: they are only mock thoughts. If Schiller's *Don Carlos* were to be regarded as a piece of history then to a large extent the drama would be false. But a work of fiction is not meant to be taken seriously in this way at all: it's all play. Even the proper names in the drama, though they correspond to names of historical personages, are mock proper names: they are not meant to be taken seriously in the work. We have a similar thing in the case of an historical painting. As a work of art it simply does not claim to give a visual representation of things that actually happened. A picture that was intended to portray some significant moment in history with photographic accuracy would not be a work of art in the higher sense of the word, but would be comparable rather to an anatomical drawing in a scientific work. The logician does not have to bother with mock thoughts, just as a physicist who sets out to investigate thunder will not pay any attention to stage thunder.

There is a world of assumption here, perhaps catastrophic, surely not accidental. The specific and thunderous identification of seriousness with truth, and of truth with what is assertible, is as pointedly put into question in Austin as it is in Derrida.

To show that this identification of seriousness is indeed an interpretation, hence not necessary and universal, is the point of Austin's going on to challenge the interpretation of seriousness (or "profundity") as the sacramental ("the outward and visible sign. . . . of an inward and spiritual act"), a challenge unprecedented (and unrepeated), so far as I know, within analytical philosophy. But so formidable is, or was, Frege's authority that Austin could not challenge his interpretation of seriousness without seeming (to that select group for whom discussion of the purport of any utterance whatsoever is a commonplace, Austin's professional audience) to be challenging the necessity for philosophical seriousness. So he says, or semi-says, "Surely the words must be spoken 'seriously'. . .," using, while desperately flagging, a qualification that his entire work on performatives is meant to call into philosophical question. Whatever the mantle Austin fantasizes his philosophical work as "dismantling," it is one of fire. Let us be careful with it.

Skepticism and the Serious

I have criticized Austin's views at length for their fateful rejection of the threat of skepticism, or let us say their exclusion of it. In a word—to tap archeological layers of *The Claim of Reason*—my criticism has been that Austin's way of rejecting skepticism's pressure amounts to a refusal to see the possibility of the repudiation of ordinary concepts by, as it were, themselves. In my lingo—following an interpretation of Wittgenstein's response that I have pressed and that I realize remains controversial—this means failing to see our possibility of repudiating our agreement in terms of which words have criteria of relation (to the world, of the world) given them in the human life form. But this means failing to see the impotence in words that skepticism fastens upon and the simultaneous power compacted in those same words of a natural (that is, of a culture's) language, that they, for example, are unpredictably and indefinitely (discontinuously, I tried saying earlier) projectible into further (not-old, not-new) contexts. (There is no *place* that words fail to reach; this does not mean that they go places limitlessly.)

But to say that Austin does not consider this route to understanding how the skeptic can (seem to) mean what he says—to be serious in his paradoxical claims—is to sense Austin in rather the opposite way from that in which Derrida tends to sense him, as expressed in this pair of hesitant, general formulations: "Does the quality of risk admitted by Austin *surround* language like a kind of *ditch* or external place of perdition which speech could never hope to leave but which it can escape by remaining 'at home,' in and by itself, in the shelter of its essence or *telos*? Or, on the contrary, [as Derrida affirms, and takes Austin to deny] is this risk rather its internal and positive condition of possibility?" ("Signature Event Context," p. 17). On the contrary, the imps of language are all over Austin's house and lot, and he knows it, even if he has not very much to say about it, as in "Other Minds" (p. 88): "'Being sure it's real' is no more proof against miracles or outrages of nature than anything else is or, *sub specie humanitatis*, can be. If we have made sure it's a goldfinch, and a real goldfinch, and then in the future it does something outrageous (explodes, quotes Mrs. Woolf, or what not), we don't say we were wrong to say it was a goldfinch, *we don't know what to say.* Words literally fail us: 'What would you have said?'" (Let's not rush to interpret this moment, for example, as casting possible failures of language into a ditch of miracles. Austin is here imagining the failure of language in a case of knowledge, and of knowledge in an exemplary case. What could be more internal to language?) A bit like the Marquis in Renoir's *Rules of the Game,* Austin doesn't want poachers and he doesn't want fences; unlike the Marquis he sees to things himself (in ordinary language procedure, there is no appeal beyond oneself: if, as well may prove to be the case, you find a mismatch with others, it is up to you to see what is to be said about this, and something had better be); he puts his humor on the line, his tone.

This may be found philosophically insufficient. I find it so, while I take its implications to go beyond any current appreciation I know of. What is at stake is not simply an exclusion but a theory of exclusion, or a place for one, and a theory at the same time of seriousness. It takes non-seriousness to be a declaration of self-exclusion (as if Iago, and not Othello, is the image of the skeptic). This is dangerous political terrain. Is the implication that to be non-serious is to be a parasite? Is it chance that this sounds like a criticism famously leveled at Weimar intellectuals?

That such criticism is dangerous, and is pertinent to Austin's work, is inscribed by Austin in a startling diagnosis, or term of criticism, he offers of philosophy's institutionalized dismissal of the subtlety, complexity, and diversity of ordinary words. I refer to a sentence in the introductory chapter of *Sense and Sensibilia:* "It is essential, *here as elsewhere* [emphasis added], to abandon old habits of *Gleichschaltung,* the deeply ingrained worship of tidy-looking dichotomies" (p. 3). Rather than demanding exclusion, Austin is here struggling against it, indeed against the most famous of the historical nightmares of exclusion, the Nazi policy of coordination, elimination of "tidy-looking" differences. Is Austin serious in assigning, however rhetorically, philosophy's organizational requirements to a wish for fascistic mastery?

Austin first offered the lectures in question in 1947. His experience in World War II in British Intelligence concerned with German affairs was known to have left various traces in his later life. Am I making too much of it? Let's be reasonable and ask what Austin proposes to *do* about seriousness, I mean how he envisions shaping people up. Is it, after all, however rhetorically, to call the police? *Is* this what the order in ordinary language comes to—an obsession with the proper, with property, with propriety? Where is the fun in that—which is something Austin claimed to be returning to philosophy?

Staying with *Sense and Sensibilia*, the first—and I think the guiding—question Austin explicitly and repeatedly raises about the doctrine he is going to discuss, exemplified by Ayer's presentation of various skeptical views, is how *seriously* it is meant. I have said that Austin's idea is that it *cannot* so be meant; this is perhaps why he feels justified in choosing Ayer's writing as his "stalking-horse," rather than choosing, say, that of Descartes or Berkeley (or Heraclitus, who Austin also suggests held the doctrine). But my question now is: What does Austin do? To "dismantle a doctrine" is what at the end he implies he has wished to accomplish. Others have felt, I believe, that this is a technical term for a wish to annihilate, and not very impersonally, or philosophically, either. But my question is still: How does whatever he does constitute a criticism of unseriousness? I assume it is by exemplifying seriousness.

Does this mean exemplifying thinking and writing that mean everything they say? And does this mean exhausting or reducing the possible significance of each of their marks? To the extent these pictures makes sense, I think we are bound to say they make no sense. I would like to say that Austin's exemplification of seriousness takes the form of showing that he can listen. This is hardly an original claim for a philosopher. It is as immediate a description of the moral of the dialogue form as is the more familiar claim of philosophy to argumentative acumen, a point demonstrated most vividly in our era by Wittgenstein's *Investigations,* with its continual fragments of dialogue. The claim is apt to be insufferable (especially—perhaps—when it is true but restricted, as in Austin's case). And Austin has suffered the consequences—or so I understand the current near-oblivion into which his name has fallen, except for the work on performatives, perhaps primarily given the life it has in literary circles by Derrida's currency.

An autograph Austinianism, noting the drone of the unserious, is the turning on a mostly plain, perhaps stilted, assertion, the question: "How many things are wrong with that remark?" (Perhaps it was a favorite Oxford examination question. The case at hand is the remark, "Well may the animal be called a pig for it certainly eats like one"; *Sense and Sensibilia,* p. 41, note.) In an Austinian frame of mind one can feel roughly this way about the questions with which Derrida opens "Signature Event Context": "Is it certain that to the word *communication* corresponds a concept that is unique, univocal, rigorously controllable, and transmittable: in a word communicable?. . . One must first of all ask oneself whether or not the word or signifier 'communicate' communicates a determinate content, an identifiable meaning, or a describable value." Now of course Derrida also thinks there are, let's say, innumerable things (but a system of them) "wrong" with these questions, and a wrongness having to do with an imperative to seriousness. (That is, his question implies that someone, or just about everyone, has been saying that it is certain that words correspond to unique, univocal, and so on, concepts. He might have heard something of the sort from Kant, or from Frege.) So it is a problem for me to understand how Derrida imagines Austin to be captured in the questions; and it is accordingly a problem for me to understand how his and Austin's struggles against such questions are allied and hostile.

That something is amiss in Austin's problematic of the serious shows itself in his use of the *Hippolytus.* He takes it, as said, as an example ("gratifying to observe") of "how excess of profundity, or rather solemnity, . . . paves the way for immorality . . . [by providing] Hippolytus [when he says "My tongue swore to, but my heart did not"] with a let-out, the bigamist with an excuse for his 'I do,'" and so on, leading up to the idea of our word as our bond. But now the words of Hippolytus would have paved this way for himself only had he planned the step of using them as an excuse. Whether or not he had, the fact is that he does not use them so—does not use them in that speech act, if saying so helps—that, on the contrary, he is incapable of breaking his promise not to reveal his knowledge of his step-mother Phaedra's ungovernable passion for him. It is exactly the consequence of this fact (is it a character flaw?) that the ensuing tragedy triples, or say generalizes, drawing Hippolytus and his father, Theseus, to their deaths after Phaedra's. So that in drawing, on the basis of the *Hippolytus,* the moral that *our word is our bond,* Austin rather fails to appreciate the case in which that motto is more a curse than a sensible maxim.

How could he have failed in this case? Shall we say that in his very seriousness about seriousness Austin fears the case in which the claim to seriousness will be abused?

I think there is more to it. If Austin has for a moment forgotten the events of the *Hippolytus* that is, I have to imagine, because of something specific to them he would like not to remember. A good possibility is the terrible, ungrantable wish Theseus madly expresses to Hippolytus:

> If there were
> some token now, some mark to make the division
> clear between friend and friend, the true and the false!
> All men should have two voices, one the just voice,
> and one as chance would have it. In this way
> the treacherous scheming voice would be confuted
> by the just, and we should never be deceived.   (ll. 924–931)

If we pick the case of Wotan as another in which making a word your bond causes the downfall of a royal house (to say the least)—out of nothing more than what will seem narcissistic requirements—then we might take as its polar opposite the case of Don Giovanni, in which all a man's words seem to take the form of promises and none of them to have the constitution of bonds. (It suggests itself that these figures are causes for opera because it is in opera that humans are shown to have at all times more than one register in which their words are uttered, so that the question of the relation between what is said and what is heard, hence the question of who utters, hence of sincerity, is continually posed.)

It is because of such an intolerable pair of possibilities that Austin may be understood to have been drawn to and alarmed by this play of Euripides, in its study of the unfathomability of sincerity. (That there are no marks or tokens—to use the terms of Theseus's wish—by which to distinguish the genuine or real from the false or fake is a way of putting Wittgenstein's discovery (according to me), alluded to a while ago, that there are not what he calls criteria for distinguishing reality and dream, or, I add, animate and inanimate, or sincerity or seriousness and hollowness or treachery, hence no way of *blocking* the threat of skepticism.)

However the cases of joking and writing poems and mouthing soliloquies have come to work themselves into the picture, there are cases more to the serious point of speaking non-seriously—cases as it were more Austinian. These would be instances, for example, of speaking in distraction or thoughtlessly or impatiently or out of pique. More to the point, that is, as excuses for having put unfortunate words into the world. Moreover, joking or writing a poem are in any case not so much excuses as banal, face-saving alternative descriptions of what was said or done. Why must such face-saving at all costs be overthrown? In part because of Austin's vivid sense of the banal and tragic understandings in which reason and reasonableness may be overthrown and the nightmare of consequences must run its course in order for the conditions of reason to reappear. In part because of Austin's detection of descriptivism, or mock cognitivism, at the root of the interpretation of the seriousness of utterance with which he aligns the interpretation of Frege's version of verism—namely, that its seriousness consists in its being "the outward and visible sign . . . of an inward spiritual act"

(p. 9), which is the dictionary definition of a religious sacrament. A tendency to identify seriousness with the sacramental implies for Austin two disastrous intellectual consequences: first, it makes "I promise to" (to take what Austin calls the awe-inspiring performative) descriptive, thus negating Austin's philosophical effort in the theory of the performative; second, it makes the truth of the description a matter of religious faith (to say the most) rather than of mundane credit.

Either of these identifications of intellectual disaster shows the concept of intention not to be, contrary to Derrida's reading of Austin, Austin's idea of what controls the understanding of utterance—neither in the mundane cases whose bond just is precisely that words outrun what you may intend or want; nor in the religious, where intention is indeed a separate act, but one which outruns the reach of ordinary understanding. Austin's positioning of his philosophical enterprise concerning performatives against a religious doctrine in his introductory chapter to *How to Do Things with Words* thus repeats the gesture in his introductory chapter to *Sense and Sensibilia* of positioning his philosophical enterprise concerning perception and certainty and presence against a doctrine of politics. That Austin's is a species of Enlightenment doctrine should not come as news. Does it follow that his championing of the ordinary is a championing of the secular and the liberal? An answer might be: Only to the extent that religion and politics are essentially detractors of the ordinary; which perhaps means, only to the extent that they are metaphysical.

Then why couldn't Austin have drawn as the plain moral of "the plain saying that *our word is our bond*"—rather than attempting to track insincerity to its metaphysical roots, to attack metaphysics as an excuse for, a cover for, insincerity—the fact that promises may sometimes rightly be broken, that our word is *no more than* our bond, that our bond is sometimes forfeit? Cannot an enlightened world run on this basis, even though we do not—sometimes should not or must not— redeem all the words we pawn?

But one may feel that our utterances are unredeemable, irretrievable, cursed; that if my word is my bond and I forfeit my bond, then since no word is really mine to dispose of as I wish (for example, by working on my intentions), what I forfeit is language itself. Philosophers have said—my parents said—that if you do not keep your promise (or was it, if you tell a lie?) people will not take your word again. That frightened me more than the idea that some person would not accept my future promises. I felt it meant that I would become unintelligible, that the words I would give in my utterances would become ungraspable, not receivable, not currency. (All words so given become misgivings.) Forfeiting my word when my word is my bond would be like forfeiting my body. Then if there is still law, and my body is still readable, it must be a new law. "I'll have no speaking, I will have my bond" [*Merchant of Venice*, 3.3.17]; Shylock correctly linked the forfeiture of the word as bond with the end of his worldly language, but his others have the power to go on talking, talking law.)

I have explicitly kept open the matter of explaining Austin's "forgetting" of so signal a fact about the *Hippolytus* as that its title character never breaks his word. The apparent lapse is surely tied up with a fact that is too ecstatic in its possibilities not to mention but whose specific implications I cannot now follow up—including some explanation of how I had until recently all but forgotten it—the fact that the very line Austin quotes and calls a "classic expression" is also quoted in Plato's *Symposium*. (Alerted to this, I have also learned of other occurrences I had forgotten, and of some I never knew.) Socrates cites it about halfway through the text, as it becomes his turn to speak, using it as an excuse, and specifically as one which he happily and ironically thereupon gives over, but an excuse to get out of speaking rather than one to get out of keeping silent. So Austin was evidently quoting and inscribing at least the *Symposium* as much as the *Hippolytus*. Can one not want to know why? My immediate guess as to what Austin wanted to forget is that the saying of words is not excusable the way the performance of actions is; or in a word, that saying something is after all, or before all, on Austinian grounds, not exactly or merely or transparently doing something. So Austin's theory of excuses cannot after all be incorporated tidily into the theory of performatives, hence releases its grounding thought—that in certain critical instances saying something is doing something—into the open again.

Two Pictures of Communication: Assigning

What I described a moment ago as Shylock's forfeiture of language takes us back to the issue of communication and hence back to the beginning of "Signature Event Context," as Derrida sets up the concepts within whose field of self-determinations Austin, so interestingly different among philosophers, is nevertheless drawn into the old philosophical griefs.

I provisionally understand Derrida's text to contain, and pit together, two pictures (using again Wittgenstein's term of diagnosis) of communication, or of my dual implication in, as it is said, using language, sending it forth from here: a picture (perhaps more than one) of emitting or transmitting and one (perhaps more) of bonding; pictures of ridding myself of an attachment and ones of retaining my attachment. On Derrida's account, the matter with the first is its dependence on an unexamined (or falsely realized) concept of what is transmitted, that is, a meaning; the matter with the second is an unexamined concept of the medium of transmission, call it writing. (Again for future reference, and to make a piece of my present context clearer, I note that Wittgenstein's diagnosis according to which in philosophy we may find that "A picture held us captive" bears measuring with Lacan's (structural?) idea of captation by an image ["The Fluctuations of the Libido," pp. 180, 182]. If one has found Lacan's division of registers among the imaginary, the symbolic, and the real to have surprising weight, then it is worth saying that Wittgenstein's *Investigations* is more scrupulous and persevering in its distinction among what seem to be just these registers than any other text I know within the analytical tradition. But of course I do not know to whom this is worth my saying.)

In the light of these competing pictures, the interest to Derrida of
Austin's work on performatives seems to be twofold: first, Austin rejects
the idea of meaning as a something that is transmitted (as it were with
nothing lost and nothing gained); second, he associates the medium of
prolongation or purloining or deferring with the concept of the signature. Further, on Derrida's account, Austin is on the right track in
contrasting meaning with force, but on the wrong track in thinking of
signing as tethering yourself (your intention) to a text. I begin with the
right track.

To indicate Austin's attention to a semantic domain ("Signature
Event Context," p. 1), or a concept of communication, that is not purely
semiotic, linguistic or symbolic (compare ibid., p. 13)—and with an
initial bow to Austin—Derrida begins his analysis with a provisional
"recourse to ordinary language," a recourse instructing us "that one
can, for instance, *communicate a movement* . . . or that . . . a displacement of force can be communicated—that is propagated, transmitted.
We also speak of different or remote places comunicating with each
other by means of a passage or opening. What takes place, in this sense,
what is transmitted, communicated, does not involve phenomena of
meaning or signification." And when Derrida turns to Austin, this
analysis prepares the list of reasons he gives for attending to (and
passing beyond) the problematic of the performative: "Communicating, in the case of the [relatively new category of communication of
the] performative . . . would be tantamount to communicating a force
through the impetus of a mark." For this and related reasons Derrida
suggests that "it might seem that Austin has shattered the concept of
communication. . . . The performative is a 'communication' which is
not limited strictly to the transference of a semantic content that is
already constituted and dominated by an orientation toward truth"
(pp. 13–14). I have already expressed my sense, counter to Derrida's, that
the association of meaning and force in Austin is precisely not to detach
the work of performatives from a relation to facts (and criteria for
identifying them). Here I note that "force" seems intuitively at least as

vulnerable to the picture of the "already constituted" something-or-other undergoing transmission as "meaning" is, and this would seem to have ruled out Austin's analysis from the outset as a genuine departure from the classical philosophical account of writing that Derrida challenges. But there is a further reason, perhaps the most important, for Derrida to wish to rule out, or limit, Austin's originality, namely, its requirement of "exhaustively defined contexts," one of whose essential elements or "organizing center remains *intention.*"

The picture of an "organizing center" seems to me imposed on Austin's writing. Derrida asserts that "one of these essential elements [for an utterance counting as a performative]—and not one among others—remains, classically, consciousness, the conscious presence of the intention of the speaking subject." Now it is true that Austin, in a footnote, does say, "It will be explained later why the having of these thoughts, feelings, and intentions is not included as just one among the other 'circumstances' already dealt with" (*How to Do Things with Words*, p. 15)—where the other circumstances are ones having to do with accepted procedures and appropriate persons executing the procedures correctly and completely. But when Austin then goes on to draw "the first big distinction" between intentions, and so forth, and (the other) "circumstances," the force (if I may put it so) of the distinction seems counter to Derrida's description of it. Derrida apparently takes Austin's notice that the having of intentions, and so forth, is "not just one among the other 'circumstances'" to suggest that intention is more "important," something like metaphysically or logically fundamental, to the setting on of a performative; whereas Austin's caution is that the requirement of intention is, in a sense (in something like the sense of metaphysics), less important, but that for that very reason it provides room for certain famous forms of intellectual or moral corruption.

The distinction Austin draws is this: In the opening instances of performatives, if when I say, for example, "I do," it happens that the (other) circumstances are not in effect then the act (the supposed performative) was not in effect, it was not done at all (for example, it wasn't the captain who performed the ceremony but the purser); whereas if, in the later instances of performatives, when I say, "I promise" (in the canonical circumstances), I have no intention of keeping it (I have not met that particular "circumstance," or condition), even so *I have promised* (Austin phrases it, "I have promised, but"). (Austin marks this difference by listing what I called "the opening instances" with Roman letters, the "later" with Greek letters.) This seems the reverse of making intention the organizing center of the analysis of performatives, since in a sense in certain major categories of performatives it shows intention to be inessential to whether a performative is in effect. (This, by the way, provides a reasonable understanding of Hippolytus's being given his moment of disclaiming, "My tongue swore to, but my heart did not": it makes explicit the fact that this will not count (for him) as determining whether he swore, whether his words are in effect. Why, nevertheless, Austin persists in distrusting Hippolytus for the wrong reason is all the more in need of a good account.)

What (Thing) Is Transmitted? Austin Moves

Much of what has come up concerning force and intention would perhaps find greater perspicuity if we pursued an Austinian ordinary language analysis of communication a step or two further than Derrida took it. In response to the thought that "we have no authorization for neglecting *communication* as a word" ("Signature Event Context," p. 1), Derrida notes that one characteristic of the (ordinary) word is to designate non-semantic movements as well as semantic transportation, as in the instances of the communicating of a movement and of communicating spaces. That this is metaphorical is a possibility Derrida says he will not assert (p. 2). It is, I note in passing, also a characteristic of the word "move" that in the contexts "I move to" or "I move that" it forms a performative (in the class Austin calls exercitives, though he seems not to list the word), a fact suggesting that the relation between semantic and non-semantic movements or transferences is not metaphorical, or at least that we do not know which comes first and is then transferred. Derrida also remarks that "it seems self-evident that the ambiguous field of the word 'communication' can be massively reduced by the limits of what is called a *context*" (p. 2), a remark I am not sure I understand. He goes on to give the beginning of what might become an ordinary language analysis of "a communication," taking "Signature Event Context" as a communication that is, presumably, limited by the context of "a philosophic *colloquium* on philosophy in the . . . French language [which] seems to prescribe that one propose . . . communications in a discursive form, . . . colloquial, . . . oral, . . . destined to be listened to, and to engage or to pursue dialogues within the horizon of an intelligibility or truth that is meaningful, such that general agreement may, in principle, be attained." And he asks, "But are the conditions *[requisits]* of a context ever absolutely determinable?" As Wittgenstein urges, let's look and see.

Is to be informed that the context of a communication so described—as discursive, to be listened to, and so forth—is a philosophic colloquium of a certain kind, to have that information reduced in ambiguity? I suppose that the idea of ambiguity is of allowing interpretations that are definite (or determined?) enough to be competing; but to invite someone to prepare a communication that is discursive, engages in or pursues dialogue, and so on, is not yet definite enough to be ambiguous; it is perhaps vague. And isn't what's wanted to know the context? Being told that the communication is for a philosophic colloquium in the French language on communication for such-and-such an organization in Canada is likely to clarify the matter—not, however, by reducing ambiguity. Would ambiguity be reduced, once the context has determined things—or would determinateness be increased—by providing the names of every person to be present when the communication is delivered? (In the late 1960's, when university gatherings were apt to inspire a certain laxness of manners, officials at Harvard reaffirmed the rule that jackets and ties would be worn in the dining halls. So naturally a certain number of young men showed up in jackets and ties and without shirts. I do not recall that any showed up in jackets and ties and shirts and without trousers. Was the original rule indeterminate? To imagine so would be to slight the difference between disobeying the rule (by failing to wear a jacket and a tie) and mocking it (by obeying it literally and disgracefully). This, and who knows the extent of other matters, might become decisive, given certain interests.)

In the face of such possibilities, roving between the urgent and the frivolous, do I accept the question "Are the conditions of a context ever absolutely determinable?" If "conditions" is a fair translation of *requisits* (or if "requisites" is), then that question is ambiguous: Derrida, in his example, was determining the conditions that the context of a particular colloquium places on any communication it invites; he was not considering the determination of that colloquium's constituting a context for such a determination of communication. Here that part of the definition of "communication" comes in that sets up the circumstances in which delivering the communication can happen—distinct spaces have to be in place if there is to be a passage through which they are communicating (the unobstructed, opposite sides of a room do not communicate with one another, even when the acoustics between them are perfect); an institution has to be in operation for me to deliver a communication to it, that is, for it to receive such a thing, that is, for there to be such a thing to be understood.

What part does understanding play in the concept of communication? This can be taken as the question raised in *Philosophical Investigations* as early as the early builders. They may be taken as setting up the sill and door to the *Investigations*. For the builder's calls to be calls "for" certain building stones, those things must already be handy for the assistant at the communicating end. Then what happens at the other end is a function of there being an other there. The image of sender and receiver emblematizes and obscures this. The conditions of understanding are not exhaustively specifiable a priori (by, let's say, rules). A sense of limitation in the understanding between builder and assistant is a sense of limitation in the surprises they may have for each other, in their possibilities, or degrees of freedom. The capacity for understanding is the same as the capacity for misunderstanding, as the capacities for walking and talking are the same as the capacities for stumbling and stammering. (I would like to refer here to my text "Notes on the Opening of Wittgenstein's *Investigations*.")

Philosophers such as Austin and Wittgenstein are struck by the fact that in philosophy, for some reason, context seems a fragile, erasable, perhaps we can say extra-logical, feature of making sense, so that in analyzing whether and how sense is made, such a thing as intention, and a private intention at that (public space having been erased, you may say enclosed, or subjected to reduction), appears to have to do all the work of, as it were, communication. It is in such straits (straits of metaphysics) that intention is to preserve, and I would say, reattain, or represent, presence (beyond myself, to someone or something). The way Austin uses the word "present" (as in "verbs in the first person present indicative active" (see *How to Do Things with Words*, p. 5) is anything but that (metaphysically inspired) way.

For Austin as for Wittgenstein intention is anything but something inner making up for the absence of something outer; it lines the outer. Intention can guide the variation of signal flags through a sequence of positions, but it cannot—that is, *that* intention cannot—guide the establishing of the flags, and what counts as their positions, and what the positions signify, and so on. In the absence of this institution no such intention of variation is formulable. It may help to say: a context *is* what allows such a thing as an intention to do so much and to be so little. It is why some things you can do intentionally you can do inadvertently. Perhaps promising is not one of these things. Then how do we understand Hippolytus? Perhaps as having promised unbreakably yet thoughtlessly? How, according to Austin, *could* this happen? Is our difference from Hippolytus a cultural one? Psychological? Linguistic? Accidental?

Austin—importantly unlike Wittgenstein—does not contrast his use of, for example, "present" with its use in metaphysics, since he does not grant metaphysics sufficient intellectual autonomy to establish, even apparently, its own use; as if each metaphysician has found his or her own private form of mischief—not, I grant, a very satisfying diagnosis, but that failure might itself be diagnostic, for example, arise from our imposing an unsatisfying demand for satisfaction. If I just now gave enough of an Austinian analysis of communication and intention to sense its workings, its very obviousness might rather have dampened our enthusiasm for philosophy of a certain weight. This would of course be a result Austin applauds, I mean intends. Here are some more of Austin's closing words from *Sense and Sensibilia:* "The main thing is not to get bamboozled into asking [a] question at all . . . that has no answer, . . . a quite unreal question. The right policy is to go back to a much earlier stage, and to dismantle the whole doctrine before it gets off the ground."

I have suggested that Austin must take the opening question of "Signature Event Context" as a certain instance of what he calls "a quite unreal question": "Is it certain that to the word *communication* corresponds a concept that is unique, univocal, rigorously controllable, and transmittable, in a word, communicable?" Yet Austin's idea of "dismantling the whole doctrine" very clearly bears (or should be seen to bear) elective affinities with Derrida's point in constructing such a—shall we say loaded?—question. And I have repeatedly weighed in against Austin's self-image of going back to a stage before a doctrine gets off the ground; that is already too late, as the earlier pictures of our philosophical ground as strewn with ruins attests. When a moment ago I described Austin and Wittgenstein as philosophers "for some reason" struck by the erasure of context in philosophy, I was registering my sense of skepticism's work as precisely removing our access to context, to the before and after, the ins and outs, of an expression. This may be seen as part of philosophy's denial of my powerlessness (over the world, over others, over myself, over language) by demanding that all power seem to originate with me, and in isolation. And contrariwise, it may be seen as philosophy's denial of my power (such as it may be) by sublimizing the power of the world, or say nature. While Austin deplores the oblivion of context and seeks tirelessly to recall it in each case, he seeks no systematic account, either of context or of its oblivion, and seems quite ready to conclude that philosophy has repudiated its claims to intelligence. Wittgenstein does sense a systematic cause for the oblivion, or erasure of context—in a word, for skepticism—a cause that does not so much repudiate philosophy's intelligence as show ways of its repudiation of itself. But for all his decisive and original constancy in facing its power, he leaves it obscurely articulated (perhaps for sufficient reason).

The skeptical threat, and ensuing doctrines, are, or were, off the ground; and to leave this charge of negativity philosopically untraced is to invite bamboozlement. At the same time Austin's undying value, for me, is his challenge to philosophy to show, let's say, the awful reality of its unreal questions, which for me, after Austin, is to say, its origins in passages of the everyday.

Derrida's opening question, while expressing an affinity with Austin's scruples, simultaneously flaunts a certain disdain for them. I do not find that his understanding of the ordinary, as "effects" of language, that are of course to be found "every day," "the most common thing in the world" ("Signature Event Context," p. 20), justifies this tone. (The appeal, or construction, of "effect" here is to be compared with the skeptic's concession, after doing his work of repudiation, that our ordinary knowledge and perception serve well enough "of course" "for practical purposes," as if what our purposes and practicalities are are quite transparent to us. Austin is pointing to this suspicious philosophical consessiveness in saying: "There's the bit where you say it and the bit where you take it back"; *Sense and Sensibilia*, p. 2). Reciprocally, Austin's understanding of philosophy's self-entanglement, or self-mantling, as being bamboozled does not justify his incuriousness about, for example, his invoking of Euripidean tragedy. Shall I wish that the philosophical mind had not split itself?

Two Pictures of Language in Relation to (the) World

When I found skepticism to be well off the ground and taking its course in Shakespearean tragedy—always and precisely too late, tragically too late, to stop—I accounted for its appearances in such a way as this:

> In the unbroken tradition of epistemology since Descartes and Locke (radically questioned from within itself only in our period), . . . the world normally present to us (the world in whose existence, as it is typically put, we "believe") is brought into question and vanishes, whereupon all connection with a world is found to hang upon what can be said to be "present to the senses"; and that turns out, shockingly, not to be the world. At this point the doubter finds himself cast into skepticism, turning the existence of the external world into a problem. Kant called it a scandal to philosophy and committed his genius to putting a stop to it, but it remains active in the conflicts between traditional philosophers and their ordinary language critics, and it inhabits the void of comprehension between continental ontology and Anglo-American analysis. . . . The skeptic is neither the knave Austin took him to be, nor the fool the pragmatists took him for. . . . He forgoes the world for just the reason that the world is important, that it is the scene and stage of connection with the present: he finds that it vanishes exactly with the effort to *make* it present. If this makes him unsuccessful, that is because the presentness achieved by certainty of the senses cannot compensate for the presentness which had been elaborated through our old absorption in the world. But the wish for genuine presentness is there, and there was a time when the effort, however hysterical, to assure epistemological presentness was the best expression of seriousness about our relation to the world, the expression of an awareness that presentness was threatened, gone. If epistemology wished to make knowing a substitute for that fact, that is scarcely foolish or knavish, and scarcely some simple mistake. It is, in fact, one way to describe the tragedy *King Lear* records. (*Must We Mean What We Say?* pp. 323–324)

But isn't this all familiar by now, a quarter of a century later, to be comprehended as part of the metaphysics of presence? But if that metaphysics constitutes the establishing of the Western philosophical tradition, what would have to have become familiar is the origination of that structure in the (tragic) experience that—in my reading skepticism out of, let's say, the crossing of Shakespeare and Descartes—creates presence. "Creates presence," to summarize *The Claim of Reason*, here means something like: strips our criteria from ourselves and so transfigures, or disfigures, human language into a private possession, or possessor, a structure in which we are each (as Thoreau puts it) said to live, that is, to preserve ourselves (in Descartes's terms, to take over from God the task of originating ourselves, about which we are bound to get the wrong idea), a structure that is no structure (but is a building of air, or of breath, in Wittgenstein's picture of it), which we also destroy. What would it mean for this to become familiar?

I have sometimes figured that it was the thought of considering something like this question, raised by such a passage as that I just quoted from myself, that produced my invitation to Paris to meet Derrida back then. But it seems that a quarter of a century ago we did not satisfy the conditions under which—the context was not one in which—we could receive communications from one another. But couldn't I have found some words in which to try alternative interpretations of what in that passage I call assuring epistemological presentness? I say that once upon a time (perhaps for two millennia) this search for presentness expressed seriousness ("however hysterical"—a qualification that, for me, has grown with interest) about our relation to things (including others, including ourselves). I was taking it that, for the likes of me, certainty in relation to the presence of the idea of God—Descartes's solution—was not an option of seriousness. With that departure, I did, as in reading *Othello*, take it that a replacement of that certainty in relation to the presence of a finite other was a possibility; but I say, in effect, that the implication of this possibility goes beyond what I felt was to be accomplished in the terms of *The Claim of Reason* (pp. 451, 482)

After reading Derrida on Husserl I ask, from the other direction, whether I would have been prepared to think of voice as a further interpretation of epistemological authority, that is, as an *answer* to skepticism. If I had, I might not have pursued the idea of the voice, or rather of its silencing, as the *goal* of skepticism. (This would be why, as an answer, voice comes too late; Desdemona is suffocated; Cordelia is hanged, and the last thing Lear looks upon, as it was about the first thing we knew he cared about, is her mouth.) I was carrying around Wittgenstein's exchange with himself: "Do I myself not see and hear myself, then?—That can be said. . . . My own relation to my words [that is, to my utterances] is wholly different from other people's" (*Investigations*, p. 191). It might have played a premature role either in dissuading me from listening for a metaphysical voice or in prompting me to ask: If not via the obvious sense organs, then what *is* my relation to my voice?

Here is an apt invitation for the mythology of Beethoven's deafness to break in, pressing the question: What is it to hear music? In this context, or irruption, the question means: What is it to hear music's origin, hear it originating, what the composer hears? (That cannot be very like hearing a performance of music, even though *some* music sounds as if that were its origin. Such hearing results easily in what Emerson means by quoting instead of saying anything. And it is familiar that music sometimes quotes music.) When Schopenhauer finds that music is not the representation of the world but *is* the (will of the) world, one can understand him as finding something true of language generally, but generally all but lost to it.

It suggests itself that there is an affinity among philosophical temperaments in which a passage opens—or two passages—between the traditions of philosophy, perhaps of more consequence than all the ones blocked: one between those in either space whose intuition of the issue of language and the world is that language comes to be hooked onto or emitted into the world, and one between those whose intuition is, with some perhaps necessary vagueness, of a reverse direction, in which the world calls for words, an intuition that words are, I will say, world-bound, that the world, to be experienced, is to be answered, that this is what words are for. (How the concept of experience has been tamed from its origins in peril, adventure, we may say trauma, into a philosophical construction of "senses" is doubtless a related story.) Austin, for instance, would not have been interested, or not in the same way, in a saying that ran: Our signal is our bond.

That there is something between language and the world that is not captured in the idea of representation is the minimum that Wittgenstein's *Tractatus* captures in its idea of propositions as *showing* the logical form of reality. The implication here of silence, of, I sometimes like to say, unassertiveness, is equally fundamental in the *Investigations*. But there silence is not to be found once and for all at, or as, the limit of philosophy, but rather philosophy ever and again is to refind its silence at the limit of the human. (To go much beyond such thoughts in early Wittgenstein is not for me to do. To broach them here is to mark the beginnings of my instruction in reading, among other things, the *Tractatus* in the writing of James Conant and of Eli Friedlander.) In the formulation "What expresses *itself* in language, *we* cannot express by means of language" (*Tractatus*, 4.121), what is the "it" in "itself"? Is it something other than language, say, language's other? And is this the world? The world as a whole? The logical form of reality? In which order?

Given various allusions to the idea of a morality of speech, in relation to a perfectionist dimension of the moral life, I want to add something in view of this recent sense of affinity concerning the world-boundness of language that shows itself within the difference (within the affinity) of the philosophical traditions. The world arises at the beginning of the *Tractatus*, before, as it were, there is time for logic and language to arise: "The world is all that is the case. The world is the totality of facts, not of things." Do we ask: What was there before the world? Heidegger's question, "Why is there something rather than nothing?" which Wittgenstein is said to have found meaningful (*Wittgenstein and the Vienna Circle*, p. 68), seems to assume the world is things. As the *Tractatus* is drawing to a close, Wittgenstein remarks: "It is not *how* things are in the world that is mystical, but *that* it exists." I would like to say that if the world is the totality not of things but of facts, what there is before the world (what the world is instead of) is not nothing but is the something of chaos. The perfectionist dimension of morality, in its search for that other before whom one may make oneself intelligible, expresses the sense of moral relationship as the alternative not to immorality but to moral chaos (the madness in childhood), which the present dispensation of morality may appear to represent. This relates to my wish sometimes to say that the condition of ordinary language philosophy that interests me is its intuition of the worldboundness of language. (Bound not necessarily by *this* world; and, as performatives are meant to show, not necessarily by reference. This is worth saying if only to mark that the practice of ordinary language philosophy privileges the concept of a word as opposed to privileging the concept of a sign. This might be what the difference between my view of Austin and Derrida's view comes to. But while in *Speech and Phenomena* Derrida says, "The prerogative of being cannot withstand the deconstruction of the word" [p. 74], a false construction of the word is not a charge Derrida lays at Austin's work.)

Three Pictures of My Attachment to My Words: Signing

Go back to my recounting of "Signature Event Context" as posing or opposing two pictures of communication, that of transmitting and that of bonding, in the light of which Derrida finds Austin on the right track in associating meaning with force and on the wrong track in thinking of the prolongation of meaning in the medium of writing as tethering oneself by one's signature. To indicate why Austin's distinction between meaning and force does not do what Derrida requires of it, does indeed rather the reverse (namely, shows language to be bound by the challenge of reality even when reference and truth are out of play), I had to veer off into miniature ordinary language analyses of communication, intention, context, ambiguity, determination of concepts, presence, philosophical dismantling, epistemological authority, and the metaphysical voice. In turning now from the region of meaning to the region

of the prolongation of meaning called writing and Derrida's consideration of Austin's idea of the signature as tethering, I can do no more
than mark the following turn of a path.

Derrida, in taking Austin's use of "tethering" (an offhand use it
seems, like so much in Austin dressed casually; Derrida is certainly right
to circle it) to picture the essential work of the signature as such, places
tethering in an impossible position. Derrida introduces Austin's theme
this way: "Not only does Austin not doubt that the source of an oral
utterance in the present indicative active is *present* to the utterance and
its statement . . . but he does not even doubt that the equivalent of this
tie to the source utterance is simply evident in and assured by a
signature" ("Signature Event Context," p. 19). Austin is then cited, in
part, as follows: "Where there is *not* . . . a reference to the person doing
the uttering, . . . then in fact he will be 'referred to' in one of two ways:
. . . (b) In written utterances . . . *by his appending his signature* (this
has to be done because, of course, written utterances are not tethered
to their origin in the way spoken ones are)" (pp. 19–20). Derrida feels
he must rewarn us that "the condition of possibility of [the common
effect of signature] is simultaneously the condition of their impossibility" (p. 20). But once again, the question is as to the autonomy of
(metaphysical) philosophy, of the direction of the burden of proof of
its existence. Derrida asks for the everyday effects of signature to be
exposed as effects, that is, as functions of obeying and disobeying
conditions of something like philosophical (conceptual) purity; whereas
on the contrary (but not necessarily in contradiction) Austin asks for
the philosophical imposition of conditions on the ordinary to be exposed as impositions. It will take the work of Wittgenstein's *Investigations* to be able to say: ordinary language philosophy exposes
philosophy (in its connection with skepticism and presence) as a certain
set of effects of ordinary language, using ordinary words (what others
are there?) but stripping them of our agreement in criteria, our attune-
ment; or put otherwise, using them in such a way that their conditions
of impossibility (to block skepticism, to grant presence) are simultane-

ously their conditions of possibility (to recount a world, one shared). (This opposition is roughly what in challenging Kripke's reading of the *Investigations* on the subjects of skepticism, privacy, rules, and so on, I call the argument of the ordinary, which I say neither side must win; *Conditions Handsome and Unhandsome,* Lecture II).

That Austin's idea of tethering is specifically produced in *opposition* to metaphysical effects of presence (not as a refutation but as an exercise of freedom) is suggested in Austin's putting three pictures in play of our attachment to our words: in addition to that of the tether there is, as emphasized, that of the bond, but then also, rather passed by, that of the shackle (*How to Do Things with Words*, p. 10). I called attention to the ambiguity, or irony, in Austin's motto "Our word is our bond": meant to free us from metaphysics, that is, false profundity, it locks us into it, or into a parody of it. The other two terms mark the sides of the irony.

My word as bond is introduced by Austin, as I noted, in contrast to an imagined, violent interpretation of a performative—of the obligation incurred by saying "I promise to. . . ," as "[putting] on record [that is, describing, logocentrically] my spiritual assumption of a spiritual shackle" (ibid.). It is accordingly in contrast to this intellectually and morally obnoxious "excess of profundity" that Austin happily grants profundity's self-congratulatory sense of its own moral solidity and welcomes its sense of the likes of him in contrast as one of "a generation of superficial theorizers." The concept of the "tethering" of the signature is used to mark the happily contrasted superficiality in my improbable relation to my words. (This use of the rather arch "tether" is itself a moment of signature Austin, playing the Englishman, in its deflationary use of a verb. Compare: "When I say, before the registrar or altar, etc., 'I do', I am not reporting on a marriage: I am indulging in it" [ibid., p. 6].) My signature is my mark, or stamp; it is nothing purer or more absolute than my functioning body which it puts on the line, my most superficial presence; an "X" will do, say, for the deed to a mine. It will no doubt need witnessing; a signature is essentially witnessable, as by bystanders, as presumably an intention ("through and through present to itself and to its content"; "Signature Event Context," p. 18) is not. (Can an "X" mark the witness to the marking of an "X"? How about a "Y"?) Evidently the function of a (tethered) signature is to pick you out, you as your body, not in your or its absoluteness or purity (whatever this would mean) but in your relative and impure identity, not from any possible human that could exist (a mere signature would be hard-pressed to do this, but some look as if they would be pleased to) but from whom or from which you or it might need distinguishing. That there is no assurance of, or only relative finality to, human identity is an endless subject of comedy and tragedy and the law, from Homer's Ulysses and Shakespeare's twins to Hitchcock's wrong men. Shall we say that signatures "cannot" resolve the irony of human identity (that I am I, and am what I am not, and not what I am, and not what I am not), or that, like everything human, they participate in this irony, or pathos? If your interest is attracted to the former (the "cannot") you will of course want to understand why philosophy wishes otherwise. You may say that it wishes to deny that the impossibility of signature is its condition of possibility. But to whom is this communicated? Who is to be informed or convinced by it? I might say to the skeptic, "The impossibility of seeing objects is the condition of possibility of seeing them, here, there, now, gone." To which the skeptic seems invited to reply, "That's just what I think: The impossibility of seeing them absolutely, purely, etc., is the necessity of seeing them relatively, for practical purposes." Mustn't you take yourself for a skeptic to feel reassured by this?

All this about being distinguished and putting my stamp on things is part of Emerson's study of "genius"—the condition of which for him is universally distributed, which is the cause of his hectoring of his fellows (a cause of his prose, his tone) to stop quoting and start saying something, to find their voices, apart from which they do not know they exist and hence "have" signatures. Ghosts have none, so if I am a ghost my signature is necessarily forged. Moments of adolescence feel so; this is another way of seeing why Emerson's addressee—like Thoreau's, like Nietzsche's—is characteristically a youth. The question of identity is enacted in the history of America (can I say instead the United States?); old words brought to a new world. That "new" implies "old" is one of the endless threads woven into the problematic of old and new set in motion in Emerson's "Experience," as if the incessant mismatch of concept and appearance (negating *The Critique of Pure Reason*) *is* the experience of America ("new yet unapproachable"—is it before or behind us?). (Is it now true, still true, more true, that all the world is America? It would follow that there is no America to go to. Does the truth and falseness of this enter into the cause of the famous success of deconstruction in America?) The theme of old and new words was announced in the citation I earlier took from the close of *Speech and Phenomena;* it is this, I assume, that is inscribed as a collateral topic in "Signature Event Context" under the name "paleonymics" (p. 21), the logic of which Derrida says he cannot develop there—but evidently is not thereby excluding. Old words in a new world as an old theme is confronted in what still seems a new way, because of the presentness of its engagement with the past, in the always under-known *In The American Grain* of William Carlos Williams.

I suppose that it is a related superficiality Derrida is reveling in when in signing "Signature Event Context" he mocks the importance that philosophy can attach to signatures by offering to sign his communication on the spot, whereupon three different marks of his name materialize on the page—"J.D."; a facsmilie of his written signature; below that (as in a business letter), a typed or printed instance of it. If the idea is that the outburst of hysterical and obsessive repetitions— violent cats and mouses of here's and there's and this's and puns—is the appropriate (non-excessive) response to philosophy's efforts at fixation and certainty and completion, then I can imagine Austin too taking some professional enjoyment in it. Yet it strikes me—in making such fun of what are after all quite trivial virtuosities of everyday existence (like getting a few unreadable scratches quite automatically into a perfectly readable form; understanding that each can be printed in-definitely many times, the printed version but not the handwritten in many faces, not at least to the same effect; and that both can further be Xeroxed, or made into rubber stamps for perhaps others to use, resulting sometimes in forgery, sometimes in plagiarism, sometimes not, and so on)—it strikes me not as participating in but as claiming too knowing a place in the sphere of the anxiety of identity and existence that philosophy is captivated by, too much playing Poe's Dupin to the uncomprehending Prefect of the Parisian Police. (And what American am I inventing in order to think so?)

Austin's tethering is the condition of possibility for the alarming fun of Derrida's multiplication of signatures, for the hysterical-obsessive discovery—a breakdown of the distinction of active and passive—that my words fly from me *and* stick to me, that I can never (on a certain picture of a word) set my words down, leave my mark, since their burdens are not corded bales. Is this experience abnormal or perfectly normal? Let's go back to the interpretation of writing that Derrida "would go so far as to say . . . is the interpretation that is peculiar and proper to philosophy," namely, that seemingly obvious perception of writing as a *"means of communication* . . . extending enormously, if not infinitely, the domain of oral or gestural communication" ("Signature Event Context," p. 3), about which he comments: "the essential drift bearing on writing as an iterative structure, cut off from all absolute responsibility, from *consciousness* as the ultimate authority, orphaned and separated at birth from the assistance of its father, is precisely what Plato condemns in the *Phaedrus.*" Philosophy sees that writing is meant for the absent receiver/addressee, who may be dead. It fails to consider, according to Derrida, that it works equally in the face of the death of the sender/addressor. Taking Condillac as his instance, Derrida writes: "The absence of the sender . . . from the mark that he abandons, and which cuts itself off from him and continues to produce effects inde-pendently of his presence and of the present actuality of his intentions, indeed even after his death, his absence, which moreover belongs to the structure of all writing . . . of all language in general . . . this absence is not examined by Condillac" (ibid., p. 5). A direct conclusion seems to be that absolute responsibility for an essential predicate cannot be tethered to a mortal. What other brand of responsibility can be?

Near the end of my first chapter I adduced Thoreau as an example explicitly counter, in each particular, to Derrida's characterization of philosophy's inherent sense of the drift of writing. And now at the end of the present chapter I find myself wondering whether I was not too quick all those years ago in my *Senses of Walden*—in discovering Thoreau's *Walden* as a scripture, a testament, that is, written in antici-pation of his own death—when I refused to allow that this was an acknowledgment, or theory, of all writing. Such a claim seemed to me not to capture Thoreau's achievement, not to distinguish it from, say, the making of a will (a notable form of words), which is about as common as possessions. I might now say that the writing as of a testament, in view of one's death, is a description of all *serious* writing.

Thus this chapter at its end unignorably declares its own desire to understand the seriousness of philosophical prose, as it were the judg-ment of this world. Failing this, and thinking of Thoreau's (following Emerson's) perpetual standing on the line betwen ecstasy and despair (between the promise of freedom from the past and the inconsequence of accepting the promise only for oneself, call this standing for the ordinary), I take forward another step or two the cause of Austin's, at a stroke, invoking the *Symposium* as well as the *Hippolytus*.

The conclusion of the *Symposium* famously opens the question of the relation of writing tragedy to writing comedy, having along the way both inscribed Euripides' Hippolytus and incorporated a figure called Aristophanes (as Aristophanes had already incorporated a figure called Socrates in *The Clouds*, and in *The Frogs* cited the same line Austin cites from the *Hippolytus*). Not doubting Austin's knowledge of these mat-ters, I do not avoid the conclusion that Austin's reinscription of a legendary line from a tragic and a comic classic source calls attention to the comedy, often quite delirious, of Austin's own prose, and sets as a challenge the consequent question of philosophy's—hence his own—seriousness. I mention drily Austin's recurrent clowning, of course sometimes by means of groaning puns ("myth-eaten theories"), but often by twisted banalities ("better to split hairs than to start them"), and, I think most characteristically, by his slanted allusiveness across the history of English prose and poetry, from Bacon and Shakespeare to Donne and Pope and Wordsworth and Eliot. (Geoffrey Hill and, after him, Christopher Ricks helpfully gather these allusions together. Their interpretations of Austin's literariness, admiring but sometimes suspicious, deserve careful consideration.) I think of this as Austin's manner in which to take on, to keep alive, the ancient competition of philosophy with poetry, or, say, of justice and appeal. Not to weigh Austin's smacks at the non-seriousness of jokes, and poetry, and theater against the obsessiveness of his perception of philosophy's chronic *false* seriousness, is to refuse to read Austin's, well, signature.

I have elsewhere contrasted Derrida's and Austin's somewhat hysterical insistence on being initial, medial, unfinished, undefined, with Wittgenstein's punctuating readiness to come to an end, hence perhaps at any time to a dead end. Quite as if I am taking it at such times that this readiness is all that marks seriousness, in saying or doing or suffering anything.

Consider the fit of this characterization of writing (done in view of one's death, with, as Thoreau also puts it, the work of one's hands only) with Austin's characterization of his hand as tethering him to his words. As specifying the condition of Derrida's multiplication of signatures, I read Austin not as denying that I have to abandon my words, create so many orphans, but as affirming that I am abandoned to them, as to thieves, or conspirators, taking my breath away, which metaphysics would deny. (Emerson's emphasis on writing and thinking as self-abandonment is on my mind here.) Hence Austin's tethering reverses Derrida's picture of writing as *extending the limits*—or "relaxing" them ("Signature Event Context," p. 3)—of the voice or breath (as if *that* much is too obvious to mention); turns it so to speak into one of *limiting the (inevitable) extension* of the voice, which will always escape me and will forever find its way back to me. As if the price of having once spoken, or remarked, taken something as remarkable (worth noting, yours to note, about which to make an ado), is to have spoken forever, to have taken on the responsibility for speaking further, the responsibility of responsiveness, of answerability, to make yourself intelligible. The sense that once one has acted or done something one has acted or done something forever may seem, in comparison, only derivatively the stuff of tragedy, or melodrama. Talking too much is all too common; acting or doing too much seems rather the stuff of farce. All of which, again, seems incompatible with Austin's claim that excuses apply to utterances as to "all" actions.

It is in recognizing this abandonment to my words, as if to unfeasible epitaphs, presaging the leave-taking of death, that I know my voice, recognize my words (no different from yours) as mine. Austin's righteous indignation at the sacramentalizing of the work of language comes, I would guess, from his sense that this attempt to ground a word's depth in religious practice dulls the reality both of the ordinary and of disappointment with the ordinary.

Doubling an earlier question about the bearability of action, of having a body, in relation to the action of tragedy, if we now ask, "How is it that having a voice is bearable, a voice that always escapes us, or is stolen?" and "What is the nature of the force that allows language not only to mean and to state but to to work, to act?" these begin to sound like questions of opera. I was led near the outset of these remarks to a distinction between the pathos of sense, of having a voice, and the suffering of the necessity of action, the tragedy of, so to speak, having a body, unless you can find its comedy. The ground of the distinction, if it is a valid one, arises from an interpretation of the fantasy of the privacy of language (which Austin, Wittgenstein, and Derrida are all at pains to contest) as answering terrors simultaneously that we are necessarily inexpressive, unintelligible, *and* that we are expressive beyond our means, too intelligible for our good (as expressed in *The Claim of Reason*, pp. 351–352). It is a difference perhaps between hysteria and obsession, between shame and guilt, between fantasies of suffocation and ones of being torn apart. It still sounds to me like the matter of opera.

~ 3
Opera and the Lease of Voice

In memory of Judith Shklar

This ephemeral quality seemed to Benjamin the just price it [a periodical he had agreed to edit] had to exact for its striving after what Benjamin understood as true actuality: "Why according to a talmudic legend even the angels—new ones each moment in innumerable bands—are created so that, after they have sung their hymn before God, they cease and dissolve into the naught." . . . To this, however, was added for Benjamin the further conception of Jewish tradition of the personal angel of each human being who represents the latter's secret self and whose name nevertheless remains hidden from him. In angelic shape, but in part also in the form of his secret name, the heavenly self of a human being (like everything else created) is woven into a curtain hanging before the throne of God. This angel, to be sure, can also enter into opposition to, and a relation of strong tension with, the earthly creature to whom he is attached.

Gershom Scholem, "Walter Benjamin and His Angel," pp. 212, 213

When a few years ago I was asked to say how as a philosopher I had become interested in film, I replied by saying, roughly, that the inflection more pertinent to my experience was how a lost young musician had come to recognize his interests as philosophical, one whose education (in narrative, in poetry, in song, in dance) had been more formed by going to the movies than by reading books. I might have included listening to the radio along with going to the movies, since, interweaved with many other matters, broadcasts were the primary attestation I had growing up of high culture as a shared world, of ours as a reformable world, not merely endurable. Film was rapturous, as was jazz, but shareable only by marvelous chance; radio announced itself as originating from some specific elsewhere. There was, as I recall it, no Sunday after Sunday school without returning home to Toscanini and the NBC symphony; nor any long Saturday afternoon, when my mother was not herself at the radio station (vaudeville was about gone, or we were in Sacramento, out of the circuit), without the broadcast of the Metropolitan Opera, self-consciously bringing the glamour of culture to provincial imaginations. More than once, when I was listening with my father to a program called "Information Please"—on which regular and celebrity panelists answered questions sent in to stump them by listeners, on subjects from baseball statistics and the usual queries about presidents and capitals and rivers, to identification by opus numbers and identification of lines of poetry, usually from Shakespeare—my father would marvel and say, it seemed to himself: "They are the aristocracy." It is the sort of escaped remark that leaves an impression, against the inevitable battery of his counter-remarks that it had to make its way through, in the form of anxious mottoes like "You don't know the value of a dollar" or "You have to have a trade."

Twice I remember asking my mother, "Why are operas always sad?" She tried no answer, but she was someone to whom I could direct such a perplexity. I would come to give myself various answers to the question—based on questions having to do, for example, with what occasions people to sing, and what plots best allow for such occasions, questions which I would later come to feel assumed the question, not answered it. I do not know that it is the most searching question one might ask of opera, but the most interesting directions for an answer I have been given to it come from another woman, Catherine Clément in her book *Opera, or the Undoing of Women*, published in 1979, translated into English some ten years later, when I came across it. Her answer is, in effect, that opera is about the death of women, and about the singing of women, and can be seen to be about the fact that women die *because* they sing.

Evidently, whatever meanings will unfold here, the idea is meant to capture countless forms in which men want and want not to hear the woman's voice; to know and not to know what and that she desires; to know and not to know what she knows about men's desires, for example, the extent to which theirs may be feminine, when hers may or may not be; to know that she will judge favorably on our petition to exist, or that her judgment can be stopped. I came across Clément's book in the months after identifying as one form in which men must and must not hear the woman's voice, that philosophical self-torment whose shape is skepticism, in which the philosopher wants and wants not to exempt himself from the closet of privacy, wants and wants not to become intelligible, expressive, exposed. The context of the identification (as broached in "Postscript (1989)" was one that brought issues of Wittgenstein's tormented, seductive prose together with issues raised by Eve Sedgwick's reading of Henry James's "The Beast in the Jungle" in terms of what she calls homosexual panic, the text of James that I had recently adduced in thinking about a set of films I was calling melodramas of the unknown woman, thinking in particular about the sense of a man's keeping a woman in the picture who is to go unheard. These were the months in which it became clear to me that I was going to devote one of the present lectures to the phenomenon of opera. My response to Clément's manner is no less significant, while less explicit here, than my response to her conclusions. Her book is addressed, differently, to men and to women: to women collectively ("Women like me from an earlier time, come" [p. 11], "We as women will be mad together with this cotton hero" [p. 37]); to men individually, at the end with an expectant farewell ("You, my son, . . . you wanted secrecy, mystery, and shame. But . . . no doubt there are also great unthought myths hanging around in the corners of your head, whose prisoner you are. . . . Opera is the collection of these myths" [p. 178]), at the beginning in a bored gratitude ("For him the music comes first. We have had this discussion a hundred times. . . . This perfect musician is a Don Juan who has invested the enveloping nature of music with the fantasy of an ever elusive, inviolate woman. . . . I will go along with it. Lectures can be useful" [p. 13]). I might wish I had had such invitations, tricky as they are, to respond to as this man that I had become, when I started out writing about women on film. Doubtless I constructed imaginary invitations. I cannot now, in any case, as I implied, really take up Clément's provocation about opera, except to cite it as a welcome debt.

I am not at the moment interested in bringing counter-examples to Clément's claims (claims I have formulated in terms in which I have posed for myself the issue of the woman's voice)—such as that she does not mention, in her horror of most marriage, *Fidelio* and its Leonora, perhaps because Beethoven's Leonora succeeds by taking a man's role; nor give directions for explaining the apparent triumph or vindication of women in, say, *The Marriage of Figaro*, perhaps because she feels that the Count's being brought to ask forgiveness is not triumph enough to make sense of what the women have been through; nor is concerned to articulate a difference in the reasons men die, which for her must mean a difference in the reasons men sing. She is, moreover, not overly careful to justify theoretically her perverse attention to the words of opera in apparent neglect of the music, which everyone knows (does someone imagine Clément not to know what everyone knows?) to be the soul of the drama. I am more interested now to trace certain remarkable connections I seem to find between certain of her avenues to opera and mine to film.

I have been working out the thought that film—judging from the genres of comedy and of melodrama whose affinities I have traced elsewhere—is, or was, about the creation of the woman, about her demand for an education, for a voice in her history. In the comedies this happens by way of something there represented as the possibility of marriage; in the melodramas it happens in the rejection of what in them is pictured as the option of marriage. One of the films that I take as definitive of the genre of melodrama I have studied most (Max Ophuls's *Letter from an Unknown Woman*) turns upon itself in the foyer, staircase, chandeliers, and loges of an opera house (leave it to Ophuls's alluring camera) in which a performance is under way of *The Magic Flute*, with the Papageno/Papagena plot audible; as if to say—against the background of religious imagery in the film, the heroine all but identified as a nun (but shown in a place that is all but one of prostitution)—that we retain reason sufficient to recognize the imprisonment of convention but we have lost the common rituals, say of fire and water, sufficient to purify faithfulness. Mozart is, if you like, entertainment. Another of the melodramas is George Cukor's *Camille*, film's translation of *La Traviata*, in which Garbo gives perhaps her greatest performance—hence one of the greatest in the history of the medium—and confirms film as the study of the woman, whose death is shown to secure the stupefaction of men, and to carry off with it the taste for existence, the salt of the earth.

Another member of the genre, *Gaslight*, shows opera, or the voice of a woman described as a great singer, to come to the rescue of the voice, hence the sane life, of the heroine of the film, called the singer's "niece."

The film's early sequences pose the question, in so many words, whether the young woman "has a voice," which in the narrative means whether she is a promising singer, whether she has inherited her aunt's gift; but the narrative itself invites a more radical sense. Her husband's reasonably successful efforts to drive her mad are presented simultaneously as his reducing her to silence, taking away her right to a voice, and depriving her of the use of her literal inheritance from her aunt, a house and its belongings. The aunt's evidently most memorable role was as Lucia di Lammermoor (a brief tune from the opera is repeated on the sound track), and at the climax of the film the niece finds her voice in a long speech I describe as a mad song, in which, echoing Lucia, she confronts her husband with a blade. That she does not in madness actually or narratively kill this husband is in effect film's declaration of its powers in opposition to those of opera, specifically the power to provide a happier, anyway less fatal, ending.

This declaration of difference is, taken further, a sign of affinity, since opera's powers or necessities of happiness or sadness are an issue opera originally raised about itself. I think of Monteverdi's dissatisfaction with his librettist's inability to find a happy ending for *Orfeo,* generally regarded as the first masterpiece in the new medium; Monteverdi eventually, and consequentially for the development of opera, rewrote the end. For this and other reasons it no longer quite surprises me that film raises questions that would seem fundamental to thinking about opera. In acknowledging the woman's coming into her own powers (sometimes now called agency) by taking on the agency of her aunt's voice, *Gaslight* asks us to ask: Who sings, the actor, the character? And even: What is singing? What causes it?

I have been chastised for calling the niece's confrontation or denunciation of her husband an aria, as if taking theatrical speech as a metaphor for singing discounts the fact that the young woman is in fact not singing, hence disparages the achievement of genuine singing, which no musician could or should accept. Accepting this criticism as granting that I know what anyone knows about differences between speaking and singing, I imagine that it comes from a sense that I am seeking too much from the metaphor. But what I seek is the question: Since the niece in *Gaslight* (literally) takes up Lucia's instrument and scene of the blade (in a room locked alone with her hastily acquired husband), and in Lucia's context (madness as a response to being subjected to that marriage), and since Lucia is her aunt's great role, which she is now assuming, what shall we say the young woman is doing? What does she think she is doing? Something is resounding. The question of her voice is the question of her identity—specifically of how a woman inherits her identity.

The question whether she is singing is indeed the question, in reverse, most obviously asked about the so-called convention of opera, whether we are to take dramatic singing as representing speaking—take singing, namely, as *the* figure of speech. If not, how else? People on the whole do not *literally* sing to one another, at least sane people on the whole do not, exactly. They do understandably sing to themselves, under certain circumstances—more understandably than if they are heard or seen speaking to themselves. We could almost take the blatant conventionality of opera as meant to call into question the conventions or conditions making civil discourse possible—the pace, the distance, the pitch, the length, at which literal speech is supposed to take place—as though some problem had arisen about speaking as such.

Why go to film to raise the question of opera? Why not to opera directly? Well, I have in the past couple of years been experimenting with the idea that what happened to opera as an institution is that it transformed itself into film, that film is, or was, our opera. So while it is not my intention to stay indirect, I am moved to take my bearings by noting the repeated appearance opera has made over the years in my texts about film.

In the first chapter of *Pursuits of Happiness* (p. 51), broaching the connection of Shakespearean comedy with what I was calling comedies of remarriage, I cited these two sentences from Northrop Frye: "All the important writers of English comedy since Jonson have cultivated the comedy of manners with its realistic illusion and not Shakespeare's romantic and stylized kind. . . . The only place where the tradition of Shakespearean romantic comedy has survived with any theatrical effect is, as we should expect, in opera" (*A Natural Perspective*, p. 128). My immediate reason for citing this observation had been to add film to the line of a Shakespearean inheritance, but mostly for future reference, since mostly the connection I would go on to draw between film and opera was to analogize the camera's powers of transfiguration to those of music, each providing settings of words and persons that unpredictably take them into a new medium with laws of its own—each as different from theater, for example, as air from water. Both film and opera we might add at once, were discovered or invented at datable, placeable moments in Western culture; this at once makes their origins and existences both more knowable and more mysterious than those of the ancient great arts, as though a sense of the extravagant arbitrarinesses in their conventions (the raising of the voice; the displacements of the camera) needs compensating for by a metaphysical explanation of their powers.

For example, it is of significance in my account of what I call the ontology of film that the medium of the motion picture reverses the ascension in theater of character over actor; on film the actor is the subject of the camera, emphasizing that this actor could (have) become other characters (that is, emphasizing the potentiality in human existence, the self's journeying), as opposed to theater's emphasizing that this character could (will) accept other actors (that is, emphasizing the fatedness in human existence, the self's finality or typicality at each step of the journey). In opera the relative emphasis of singer and role seems undecidable in these terms, indeed unimportant beside the fact of the new conception it introduces of the relation between voice and body, a relation in which not this character and this actor are embodied in each other but in which this voice is located in—one might say disembodied within—this figure, this double, this person, this persona, this singer, whose voice is essentially unaffected by the role.

A Cartesian intuition of the absolute metaphysical difference between mind and body, together with the twin Cartesian intuition of an undefined intimacy between just this body and only this spirit, appears to describe conditions of the possibility of opera.

I think about this against the background of the credentials, as it were, I must present for my having a say in these mysteries of voice, I mean in my sense that these mysteries are in play in the loss of voice in skepticism—registered by the appearance of a simulacrum of voice in metaphysics, as I more or less put the matter in responding, in my previous chapter, to Derrida's Husserl. I think of the pair of essays that conclude *Must We Mean What We Say?* the first of which, "Knowing and Acknowledging," I quoted from in linking the idea of Derrida's sense of paradox in a word's dissociation from itself—as its way of being here and there—with skepticism in respect of the existence of others; the second of which, as if in commentary, studies *King Lear* as staging a command for the speech of three women, three daughters, which strikes the truthful, loving one as beseeching her silence, stifling her. And I have described for myself *The Claim of Reason* as opening with a reasonably pedagogical treatment of Wittgenstein's understanding of grammar and criteria as meant in such a way that we understand the possibility and the necessity of skepticism, of that level of self-doubt; and as closing with the suffocation of a woman, of Desdemona, where the path between, the path leading to and away from metaphysical isolation and fixation (causes and effects of skepticism) turns through a moment captured in Wittgenstein's *Investigations* in the idea of a private language. I call it a fantasy and articulate it as "a fear either of inexpressiveness, one in which I am not merely unknown but in which I am powerless to make myself known [and to myself]; or one in which what I express is beyond my control [which I go on to describe as betraying myself]"—so a fantasy of suffocation or of exposure (*Claim of Reason,* pp. 351–52; compare "Postscript (1989)," p. 254).

In both outcomes the fate of the skeptical conclusion—expressed as

the discovery of the fact that we cannot achieve certainty of existence—
is bound up with the fate of language, expressed as the condition of
the human voice, its being always before and beyond itself. It was in
seeming to recognize the problematic of skepticism as driving Shakespearean theater that the question became intuitive for me of a historical break in Western history in which conditions of a catastrophe of
human understanding came together, in which, for example, language
as such comes to seem incapable of representing the world. A setting
of world catastrophe is or was a fairly familiar critical sense of the
events of *Antony and Cleopatra*, a sense I share but interpret as the
advent of modern skepticism (not, of course, as *opposed* to interpreting
those events in terms of a new politics or of a reformed religion or of
the new science, possibilities taken up in *Disowning Knowledge*, pp. 20–
21). At the moment, I am interested in the fact that this play appears
within something like a year of Monteverdi's first version of *Orfeo*, in
the latter half of the first decade of the seventeenth century, the Shakespearean period also of *The Winter's Tale* and *Coriolanus*, explicitly plays
about the destruction of worlds as a function of the loss of voice (the
incoherence of one's own, the loss of language altogether), or the
inability to withstand the voices of others, as if fearing their takeover.

That Monteverdi's first opera, as well as the two that preceded his
initiating masterpiece, and Glucks's masterpiece a century later, which
brings the aria to the musical level of the recitative (a point I accept
from Joseph Kerman), all work from the myth of Orpheus and Eurydice
is almost too good to be true in establishing the myth of opera, of its
origins—the story of the power of music, epitomized as the act of
singing. So we might reemphasize the turn in the story, familiar but
not universal, in which, after moving hell to release his wife, and despite
charming tigers and stones, Orpheus at the last moment cannot redeem
Eurydice for their everyday life together again; which makes the story
one about the limitations of the power of voice. To draw morals from
myth is an ancient practice, and which moral you draw from the
Orpheus myth is apt to depend on how you understand "looking back."

A sixteenth-century Italian translator of Ovid's *Metamorphosis*, one of the sources of the myth, interprets it as "man's loss of the soul whenever he abandons reason and turns back: that is, to pursue blameworthy and earthly concerns" (*Orfeo*, ed. Whenham, p. 21). This moralism is particularly striking in view of the ease with which the moral can be seen to be about skepticism, about the loss of the world through an impossible effort to certify its existence by means of the senses, especially through looking. (Freud's observation is pertinent here, that doubt is the emotion expressive of our essential uncertainty about what is happening behind us.)

As a parable of skepticism, the myth heightens two questions raised by the Shakespearean enactments of skepticism: first, What are the conditions under which the loss of the world is figured as the loss of a wife? (true of the conditions in *Othello* and in *The Winter's Tale*, to go no further); second, Does this figuration betoken in particular that skepticism is essentially a male affair? The second issue is brought to the fore by what seems to me the banal question left by the myth—I suppose it is well realized—namely, Why does Eurydice remain silent as she follows Orpheus up the path to the light? Ovid notes that the steep path went through silent places, but are we to take it that Orpheus's pact with hell specified that Eurydice was forbidden to reassure him of her presence? We might settle for the quasi-paradox that Eurydice is showing her presence to him in the only way open to him, by his sensing her absence, which he cannot bear.

The question whether the Orpheus myth is to end happily or sadly provides us with two general matching interpretations of the expressive capacity of song: ecstasy over the absolute success of its expressiveness in recalling the world, as if bringing it back to life; melancholia over its inability to sustain the world, which may be put as an expression of the absolute inexpressiveness of the voice, of its failure to make itself heard, to become intelligible—evidently a mad state. This second option seems to be reserved for the women of opera, but only after their words can treat some difficulty internal to their marrying—in contrast to the Orpheus story, which explicitly represents the marriage as broken from outside, initially by the fatal bite of a snake, finally by a trick of the underworld. The significance in the fact that skepticism is narratively figured as an assault on marriage has been my theme since, out of the study of such assaults in film melodrama and in Shakespearean tragedy and romance, I could say that marriage, in its idea of mutual, diurnal devotion, is a figure for the ordinary, the everyday exactions of the world. This accordingly reinvokes the idea, in my opening two chapters, of metaphysics (of presence) and skepticism as opposite faces in the denial of or flight from the ordinary (as if denying it from above and from below).

〰

Before recalling instances of such marriages, or their avoidance, in opera, let us articulate a step further the concept or condition without which there is no opera, namely, that of the voice raised in song; and specifically by relating what I called the duality of the singer—the figure of the human as both necessarily and accidentally body and spirit—to the scheme of the Orpheus myth, in which the doubleness is related to the projection of the human as spanning two worlds, call them under and upper, this one and the next, or, in Kant's interpretation, the sensuous and the intelligible realms.

I am counting here on an intuition of opera which, while hard to word satisfactorily (to provide the tuition for, adopting an Emersonian thought), I imagine as widely shared, namely, that of the intervention or supervening of music into the world as revelatory of a realm of significance that either transcends our ordinary realm of experience or reveals ours under transfiguration, as if, after all, tigers can understand and birds can talk and statues come to dinner and minds can read one another. The invocation of Kant's vision of the human being as living in two worlds, or capable, as he famously expresses it, of taking two standpoints toward human existence, is meant to allow me to pursue the intuition of opera as opening the question of the passage between these worlds, which is, I hope not by chance, the region marked by what I have called Moral Perfectionism, a name that has come up, with little explanation, a time or two earlier.

Moral Perfectionism was the guiding topic of *Conditions Handsome and Unhandsome*, still occupying my mind as my thoughts were turning to opera, the region I hoped to reach in the ideas forming themselves for lectures in Jerusalem that were to begin with autobiographical reflections and the claim to one's voice. I speak of perfectionism not as a moral theory competing with the academically dominant theories of utilitarianism and Kantianism but as a dimension of the moral life that any moral theory must take account of. It is the plane on which the issue arises, "before" questions of the good and the right come to occupy moral reasoning, of the formation of moral consciousness as such, of the self as a thing of cares and commitments, one which to exist has to find itself, which underlies the myth of the self as on a journey (a path in Plato's image, a stairway in Emerson's, a ladder in others'), a journey to, let us say, the truth of itself (not exhausted by its goods and its rights). A moral advance on the journey may not be measurable from outside, so to speak, since a crisis may take the form of a refusal to yield to the acclaim of a false, or falsifying step, so that moral energy is concentrated not on motion but on constancy, of which there will be various colors, not all of them coloraturas.

That there should be these two forms of perfectionist crisis—motion and constancy, as if inertia is interpretable also as a law of human identity—is given by the self as a thing existing in perpetual relation to itself; it is to understand for itself a world in which to live, as if it must be affirmed or denied, so that while a self so conceived is characterized by the possibility of being attracted to transform the given world, it is simultaneously (barring catastrophe) attracted to the understanding of its present world as one achieved, chosen, hence as final.

If perfectionist ideas are to help us think about what opera is, what causes its singing, we must expect that opera realizes these ideas in its own ways.

In Kant's interpretation of a fundamental Platonic picture, the individual self has as it were internalized the sensuous and the super-sensuous worlds—Plato's unreal and real realms. These are now two "standpoints" which it is the condition of being human to be able to adopt in succession, in opposition to each other. In Plato's *Republic* there is a journey from one to the other beginning with a move from a sense of imprisonment and irreality (in the Cave) to a turning around of direction, that is, a reorientation, which takes one on an upward path of education under the guidance of a figure who has descended from a world of light, and so on. (In the Introduction to *Conditions Handsome and Unhandsome* I distinguish some two or three dozen features of this journey.) In Kant's *Foundations* the turn from one realm to the other takes place in every moral judgment each time you stop to think, to ask yourself your way. Nietzsche says that eternity has been cut short; in perfectionism after Kant, the journey to freedom has been cut short—to a half step—you see how to take it, where it lies, or you do not.

Kant's picture of the two worlds is meant to ground—to make intelligible—human knowledge of the human condition as constrained by morality, a constraint Kant finds to be expressed by an "ought," by the law. Emerson's contribution to perfectionism, which is for me decisive, is epitomized in his finding out how it is that we can resist what gives itself out as moral law, and yet claim to be constrained by an objective measure, a standard of the world. His counter-finding is that the moral constraint upon the human, to the human, can be expressed not, as for Kant, as an obligation, but as an attraction (or however we understand that aversive thinking which Emerson registers as the cause of society's aversion to him). Attraction as the basis of commitment—as paradoxical as taking narcissism as the basis of altruism—is at stake in the interpretation, or reinterpretation, of Freud's concept of the superego in Lacan's obscure but valuable discussion of the difference between the Ego-Ideal and the Ideal Ego (in the section of that name in Lacan's 1953–1954 *Seminar*).

I would like to explore the thought that these Kantian/Emersonian modifications of perfectionism help to tell why it is that in opera there is characteristically little elaboration of perfectionist features (which would make *The Magic Flute* exceptional). Rather we may leap, as it were, from a judgment of the world as unreal, or alien, to an encompassing sense of another realm flush with this one, into which there is no good reason we do not or cannot step, unless opera works out the reasons. Such a view will take singing, I guess above all the aria, to express the sense of being pressed or stretched between worlds—one in which to be seen, the roughly familiar world of the philosophers, and one from which to be heard, one to which one releases or abandons one's spirit (perhaps to call upon it, as Donna Anna and Donna Elvira do; perhaps to forgo it, as the Marschallin and as Violetta do; perhaps to prepare for it, as Desdemona and Brünnhilde do; perhaps to identify it with this one, as Carmen does), and which recedes when the breath of the song ends. This expression of the inexpressible (for there is no standing language of that other world; it requires understanding without meaning) I described as a mad state, as if opera is naturally pitched at this brink; and my description of this state as one of abandoning oneself is meant to recall two sites for something related to what Austin used to call philosophical field work.

One is the idea of the signature—and surely the operatic voice is the grandest realization of having a signature, the world, as Emerson puts it, wearing our color—as the sign of abandonment to your words, hence of your mortal immortality (body and spirit, father and mother according to Nietzsche). Opera may be said to absolutize this condition. (And makes counterfeit impossible, or irrelevant, since even if it were possible perfectly to impersonate this diva's voice, the impersonation would be as original an achievement as the original.) The other site is Emerson's use of the concept of abandonment to name a spiritual achievement (of, let us say, neutrality) expressed as a willingness to depart from all settled habitation, all conformity of meaning, the human as immigrant. (I guess there is no end to my wish to democratize the exclusive.) And with Emerson's abandonment I put together Thoreau's concept of our knowledge of our existence—that which proves our humanity—as, in his words, "being beside oneself in a sane sense," which I note in my book on *Walden* is the dictionary definition of ecstasy.

If this captures that quality of besideness, or, as Thoreau also calls it, nextness to a grander world than this, in the intuition of transcendence in operatic singing that I articulated a moment ago as a realm intervening, then that realm is to be understood as an irrupting of a new perspective of the self to itself. The perspective of the self to itself is an ecstatic response whose self-reflectiveness suggests the structure of narcissism.

It seems to me that the concept of narcissism here is being called into play in a double intuition of singing as ecstasy and as abandonment, an intuition of its representing responses at once among the most primitive and most sophisticated of the human scale. I mean to be invoking the development of the concept of narcissism in Freud's thinking and in its elaboration in Lacan's idea of the register of the imaginary (a register invoked by Catherine Clément, who, a few years after her book on opera, published a memoir of Lacan that recounts, in effect, the easing of her fascination with his work). So I should be clear that while in speaking of primitive and sophisticated narcissism I am alluding to the problematic of primary and secondary narcissism, and the issues it raises of the formation of the ego and of the choice of love object, I am not appealing to a given explanation of narcissism—the subject is notoriously unclear. The sense of superimposed primitiveness and sophistication—reflecting the mutual impositions of the child and the adult that child has become, the stock-in-trade of psychoanalysis—encourages me to go between these aspects of the concept of narcissism and to develop separately, as it were in each direction, the sense of the spectacular vocality of opera in its aspect as orality and in its aspect as exposure or display, sometimes named seductiveness.

Take exposure first, the sophisticated direction. If we reformulate Clément's repeated formulation, that women die because they sing, to say that women's singing exposes them to death, the use of the voice to the stopping of the voice, we have to ask what their voice exposes. If we answer that it exposes their power of desire, this takes us to the theme of love and death, one not to be denied, but at this moment it might break the thread of the relation of death to communion or communication that brought opera into play at the close of the last chapter.

This idea or direction of narcissism, in its picture or structure of self-reflection, is also a figure for thinking, as in Descartes's proof of one's existence, and one's alone, except God's—a turn toward the self that at once preserves itself and stays the vanishing of the rest of creation. And Narcissus came up for me, in entering the last part of *The Claim of Reason,* as a figure of the skeptics's desire to remain in control of his answers, a desire that makes his answers echoes, new existences of course, but not new enough. Then perhaps it is reasonable to answer our question of the risk of the woman's singing by saying that it exposes her as thinking, so exposes her to the power of those who do not want her to think, do not, that is to say, want autonomous proof of her existence.

The most precise, appropriately defiant, announcement I think of in opera of the fact of thinking as narcissism, of its exposure in or as defiant seduction, is Carmen's "Seguidilla," sung and danced in the face, and flames, of Don José's possessiveness and conditions. José: "I forbid you to speak to me"; Carmen: "I didn't speak to you . . . I sing for my own pleasure, / And I'm thinking . . . It's surely not forbidden to think." I have suggested elsewhere (in "Psychoanalysis and Cinema"), in connection with Freud's treatment of Dora, that in a certain setting on of skeptical doubt, what men want of women is to know (and not to know) what women know. Carmen is acting on this knowledge.

But can her Seguidilla really be part of this opera's acknowledgment, one among many no doubt, of what singing is—part of a luring medium's ongoing discovery of itself? Or is it simply a local artifact of this woman's character in this structure? Since Nietzsche declares, not unwickedly, a preference for *Carmen* after a lifetime of Wagner and his possessiveness and conditions, I just note the number of times a Wagner character—for example, throughout the *Ring*—is described in Wagner's stage directions in terms such as "absorbed in gloomy brooding," or "as if awakening from a deep reverie" (which I take to indicate dream-thoughts under translation). Wotan describes this to Brünnhilde most fatefully: "What lies in my breast unrelated / It must remain unspoken forever; / Myself I talk with, telling to thee" (*Die Walküre*, Act II, Scene 2. This old-fashioned translation pretty well abandons English in its effort to preserve Wotan's sense of speaking to his daughter as unhearable self-reflection.)

Before offering another line of evidence on this sophisticated side of narcissistic singing, the side of its display or exposure, I note that I am counting on a parallel development on its primitive side, the side of singing's orality, yet still a development of, let's say, intellectual agency. This confidence is based on a consideration of Freud's dense paper with the title "Negation"—that apparently endlessly determinable attribute of human thought and conduct—in which Freud reports his finding that

> the study of judgment affords us, perhaps for the first time, an insight into the origin of an intellectual function from the interplay of the primary instinctual impulses. Judging is a continuation . . . of the original process by which the ego took things into itself or expelled them from itself, according to the pleasure principle [p. 239]. . . . Expressed in the language of the oldest—the oral—instinctual impulses, the judgment is: "I should like to eat this," or "I should like to spit this out." That is to say: "It shall be inside me" or "It shall be outside me." . . . The original pleasure-ego wants to introject into itself everything that is good and to eject from itself everything that is bad. . . . The antithesis between subjective and objective does not exist from the start [p. 237]. . . . The polarity of judgment appears to correspond to the opposition of the two groups of instincts which we have supposed to exist. Affirmation—as a substitute for uniting—belongs to Eros; negation—the successor to expulsion—belongs to the instinct of destruction [p. 239].

If we accept that everything that is good and bad—the "internal" and the "external"—is everything that instinctually motivates judgment, and accept that the world is everything that is judged to be the case, then the oral, primitive basis of judgment amounts to the judgment of the world, its affirmation or negation in each utterance or outcry. (Say that the apple taken from the tree of the knowledge of good and evil represents in its orality the birth of judgment as such. Then we seem to have a hint here about why opera so attunes itself to moments of separation, as if this is the founding trauma of human experience. If we conceive that singing, in its breaths, incessantly draws in and lets out the world as such, are we not conceiving that there is no world-changing creation that is not a consequence of destruction? I am glad, further, to be reminded here of my pleasure, early in *The Claim of Reason*, in finding that Wittgenstein's development of his signature term "criterion" out of its twin, the ordinary word "criterion," keeping the ordinary schematic structure intact, could be understood as his recognizing the fact of valuing as coeval with the value of asserting fact, since ordinary criteria are bases for evaluation—for admitting or rejecting, say including and excluding—and Wittgensteinian criteria are bases for relating the world in words, or as Kant puts the matter, "applying concepts in judgments.")

It is here that a further Kantian concept might be expected to come into play, that of speaking with a "universal voice," a concept that I have invoked variously in my work early and late. I note its importance only in passing now, since to do it justice in its conceivable connection with opera would be to show how to reconcile the necessity in Kant's universality with the utter contingency of its being just this voice, out of all the others there are (not all possible others, no doubt), in just this body, that invokes the realm of, let us say, universal reconcilability, Kant's realm of ends. This intersection of the universal as found in the speaking of one who has reached, and demands, his or her individuality is Emerson's endless theme. Kant relates the possibility of aesthetic judgment (as opposed to the mere expression of taste), the rendering of words that claim universal assent upon no more than subjective grounds (in that sense enter a disproportionate or exorbitant claim), to the predication of pleasure without a concept. Think of this as assertion without a priori (transcendental) assurance that it is well grounded, grounded in the conditions of understanding or of reason—as must be the case with those concepts that assure us of a world, concepts such as substance and causation, and those ideas of reason that assure us of a moral universe, ideas such as the moral law and freedom of the will. In the realm of the aesthetic, by contrast, the feeling, as it were, comes first (Emerson calls it Intuition or Instinct), and its putative grounding concepts (the reasons for the judgment) await determination in, let me say, acts of criticism (Emerson calls them Tuitions). The point of this contentious summary is to propose that we think of the voice in opera as a judgment of the world on the basis of, called forth by, pain beyond a concept. The disproportion in the claim to share pleasure and that to share pain are not apt to coincide. It cannot be demanded of you to take events as hard, and as far, as Desdemona, Aida, Verdi's Leonora, Carmen, Brünnhilde, the Marshcallin, and Melisande do. But it can be made irresistible for you to listen and to understand beyond explanation. Then what is comic in opera? Perhaps it lies in affirming the thought that whatever causes happiness does not occur in the absence of pain, or the thought that the world may for a moment be found to escape judgment altogether. Such thoughts would suggest the affinity of Shakespearean romance with opera.

(As a marker for those with a taste for such paths, I note, without comment, a signature moment in Heidegger, from his "Letter on Humanism," in which thoughts of thinking and of what thinking is of, or belongs to—a beyond or other of our present dispensation—are thought together with the idea of listening [taking it that in the German *gehören* belonging and hearing belong, or are to be heard, together], hence within earshot of the voice, call it the hum of things: "Thinking is of Being inasmuch as thinking, coming to pass from Being, belongs to Being. At the same time thinking is of Being insofar as thinking, belonging to Being, listens to Being.")

I hear a version of primitive narcissism, a self's judgmental forming of itself, as something to be further possessed or to be overcome, in Emerson's formulation: "Character teaches above our wills. Men imagine that they communicate their virtue or vice only by overt actions, and do not see that virtue or vice emits a breath at every moment." I understand this not as meaning that we are at every moment following or breaking a rule, or that we are applying or failing to apply to ourselves the moral law, or that men are keeping a running computation of the net balance of utility that their actions are bringing to the general lot. I understand the sign of our virtue and vice to be made by the fact of our somehow judging at every moment, incessantly affirming or denying, since we are judged by our judgments (except when we judge not, that we be not judged), in which the heart is revealed. This reading leans somewhat on the shift in Emerson's sentence from the idea of communicating "their virtue or vice" to that of "virtue or vice" emitting breath, as if before the personal gets into the picture there is a general circulation of something already taken into themselves. The appearance of breath in Emerson's articulation flags the dimension of orality, the depth of talking; and the use of "character," as always in Emerson, signifies human individual formation simultaneously with the forms of writing. So the whole statement of character as at every moment emitting breath contains a theory of writing that is the counter to a theory—or to a picture—of intention. According to Emerson's counter idea we write beyond ourselves (we cannot at every moment, if at any, smell our own breath), to an effect we do not see; our beyond is not eventual but always, not the result of emission but the fact of it. How our thoughts return to us—how their return is our recognition of them as ours—is the study of what presents itself to Emerson as a theory of reading, a matter of being measured by the standard (the page) of the true man, who reflects our rejected (perhaps emitted) thoughts back to us with a certain alienated majesty. (I present this view of Emerson's theories of writing and reading in a little more detail in "Being Odd, Getting Even.")

∼

Such are the jigsaw shapes of intuition I have to propose about what singing betokens—about what conditions to look for under which the culture of the West came to ponder the powers of the human capacity to raise the voice. These are elements of a discourse that cannot hold together—that is, will be useless—apart from its conceptual funding of the experience of individual works of this institution.

The instances will have variously to specify, summarizing my shapes of intuition, the singing in opera as calling back the world, or as expressing its inexpressible abandonment; and singing as (dis)embodied within the doubleness of the human expressed as ecstasy—being beside oneself, perhaps in joy, perhaps in grief—a doubleness taken in the sense of singing out of a world in which a world is intervening, one to which perhaps we belong in abandoning ourselves. This presents singing as thinking; thinking as narcissistic reflection; narcissism as capturing both the primitiveness of singing's orality and the sophistication of singing's exposure and virtuosic display. The exposure is to a world of the separation of the self from itself, in which the splitting of the self into speech is expressed as the separation from someone who represents to that self the continuance of the world—a separation that may be figured as being forced into a false marriage. The excruciation or absoluteness of this separation seems to partake both of the terror of separation in infancy (the level of primitive narcissism, where the scream in which Wagner heard the origin of singing is still audible), and of a separation from possibility figured by the loss of the one who had descended from the realm of light, in whom one's expectation of intelligibility has been placed, and collapses.

In now going on, keeping in mind Carmen's clarification, to sketch instances from five further operas, I take ones, it turns out, in which women are thinking about how to manage a marriage, that is, how to keep its idea intact; or how to avoid one. They are from Mozart's *Marriage of Figaro*, Verdi's *Il Trovatore* and *La Traviata*, Wagner's *Götterdämmerung*, and Debussy's *Pélleas and Mélisande*. The order is chronological, but the first conveniently takes up where the later *Carmen* left off, explicitly with thinking.

Why, it has occurred to me to ask myself, are the opening words of the opening voice of *The Marriage of Figaro*—Figaro's, in his duet with Suzanna—those of a man counting? "Cinque . . . dieci . . . venti . . . trenta . . . trentasei . . . quarantatré." I believe that so far as some version of this question has seemed of interest it has been taken as showing the man's practicality and his pleasure in the fruits of his ambitious talents, in contrast with this woman's pointed interruptions demanding attention to the narcissistic measures she is taking before a mirror. Aren't men and women like that? But mustn't the passage also be heard as an opening declaration of Mozart and his great librettist da Ponte that there is no a priori limit to the resources of music in setting unpromising words into dramatic orbit, although it takes genius to demonstrate this by offering a libretto beginning with arithmetic. (Leporello's important list of women in *Don Giovanni* reaffirms the point.) It also distinctly matters to me that the action accomplished with these words is that of counting, since counting, as an interpretation of Wittgenstein's concept of a criterion has played so decisive role in my sense of Wittgenstein's *Investigations*, specifically in my defense of it as a kind of critique of skepticism, showing skepticism's possibility and its necessity. This is no time to contemplate opening a discussion of skepticism and the comic voice, but a glimpse of the issue may be taken in thinking of Leporello's list not as one of victories but as one of losses, an unfunny parody of human existence—male existence?—as requiring proof.

But now, with the display of singing as thinking, we can take the duet to be a match of two modes of thinking—the woman's narcissistic, erotically imaginative far beyond the man's worldliness; the man's at once expansive and constricted, self-congratulatory and blind—modes that intertwine throughout the opera. Such a reading at the same time continues to determine the concept of singing as the thinking that confirms existence, opening Figaro's calculations of merit at the same time to a contrast with the more archaic traditions and rights, favors and trades, that Count Almaviva is counting on. But the very fact that counting, the concept of a criterion, can be taken to make language as such possible suggests to me that singing does nothing to speaking, as it were, that spoken words do not already do. It rather isolates, absolutizes, even theorizes what words do to themselves, as proposed in the idea that the voice become signature is absolutely abandoned to its song. I should add that, since this opera is notable as one in which marriages are manageable—which means, according to the relation I earlier proposed between marriage and skepticism, that the world is successfully, if momentarily, called back from its skeptical annihilation—Orpheus's role must be extended. I find it arrayed in the sound, in Act II of *Figaro*, in the Countess's bedroom, of a triad of women's voices, as it is in a trio near the beginning of *The Magic Flute*, and at the beginning of the end of *Götterdämmerung*, and near the end of *Der Rosenkavalier*. (Does the end of *Götterdämmerung* show the management of a marriage? We'll see.)

My second instance, from Act I of *Trovatore*, is the obscure moment in which Leonora runs to meet the real man whose image, as she avows, unforgettably and beyond words intoxicates her heart, as it must—according to Lacan, avowing to interpret Freud, and I think fruitfully here—in becoming the narcissistic basis of love. Her words on initially encountering the man in the shadows are "Anima mia" (My soul), and it turns out instantly and astonishingly to be the wrong brother. My suggestion is that the unretractability of these words—Leonora's abandonment to them—lodges the possibility that it was after all the right brother, or as right as the other, to whom she thought she meant to declare herself, a rightness measured by an image that is hers alone to acknowledge, a possibility that haunts the continuously astonishing events that unfold. In emphasizing the punctuation by astonishment, I am calling attention to the feature of singing as expressing the inexpressible—in loss or in discovery, and in such a way as to raise the question whether this misalignment or undoing of soul and body is an ontological or a political (perhaps politically exploited) condition.

In *Trovatore* Verdi expresses this misalignment as one in which politics becomes private, and so disappears into power, when the Count di Luna agrees to set his political rival free if the rival's beloved will give herself to him in trade. A more civilized version of this eclipse of the public is the issue of the Droit du Seigneur, the rights of the first night, in *Figaro*. In my experience of discussions of this opera this issue is treated as something of a plotted premise, not really a powerful talking point; but it is hard to imagine that one who has in mind Jules Michelet's harrowing treatment of the subject in his great book on the witch (translated as *Satanism and Witchcraft*) could feel light-hearted about it again (or for that matter about any of its modern derivatives). Catherine Clément salutes Michelet's autobiography of the witch—recurrently taking upon himself the bereft, ecstatic woman's voice—as a precursor of her story of women driven wild in opera. Michelet's account of the origin of the witch in the absolute despair reached in certain minds (mostly women's) among the serfs of the middle ages pulses in Clément's account of the sublimed cries of rage and grief and contempt in her divas, and his prose seems to me to encourage hers in its own periodic, muted screams of continuing intellectual exasperation toward men. The psychological effect of the political in producing women of strange powers driven to a frenzy of self-liberation is a directly recognizable description of Azucena in *Trovatore*.

In *Traviata*, being sketched before *Trovatore* was complete, Verdi rather reverses the stakes of the misalignment of soul and body—I sometimes think of it as the questioning of expression, of the representability of emotion—and shows the private to become public, the theft of expressiveness, of the breath of life, figured not as historical horror and political terror but as an individual woman's disease of the lungs. (*Don Carlo* is perhaps Verdi's purest instance of the theme of the political becoming private violation, in which Carlo describes and expresses Spain as a sepulchre suffocating him.) Violetta, seduced by the son's image of unique love away from her mode of independence as disdainfulness, is seduced further, further astray, by the father's image of inclusive love, back into her excludedness. But now she is exposed by her acceptance of the men's images of her as hers, stripped of the skin of defense without some measure of which the self will not preserve itself.

Here I single out a moment among the extraordinary sequence of exchanges between this woman and this so-called father, in which, having gone behind his son's back, he tortures the woman by withholding from her, in every sensitive phrase, the daughterhood he bewitches her into fantasizing. The sequence as a whole may be understood as an argument over the concept of constraint, the father expressing the Kantian ought, the woman the attraction to a world a half step away, one which there is no rightful reason to refrain from entering. The moment I refer to is that of Violetta's climactic resignation, which comes with a turn inward, thinking to herself, looking at her existence, recognizing the world's merciless, implacable judgment. Verdi begins it with a hair-raising use of the banal shift from a key in major (here D-flat) to the same key in minor: as the father Germont has descended from an F-natural to an E-flat and reaches his D-flat expecting to have found a cadence in D-flat major, Violetta tops his D-flat with a pianissimo entrance on F-flat, thus changing the mood to D-flat minor; I find the texture between the voices to be momentarily unreadable, as if the pitches of the interval of the major seventh, up from Germont's f-natural to Violetta's F-flat (an inverted half step away), are sounded together.

So important to me is the transfigurative argument at the point and over the nature of constraint that I mark it again, for the future, by calling upon another woman's voice, Julia Kristeva's in *Tales of Love:* "What if . . . the very essence of the amatory relationship [in literature and in analysis] lay in preserving the necessity of the Ideal and its detachment from the Superego?" (p. 210). (She is, I assume one is to know, boldly declaring a moral from Lacan's discussion of the difference between the Ego-Ideal and the Ideal Ego.)

My fourth instance of thinking about a marriage, to put it mildly, is Brünnhilde's Immolation scene that ends the *Ring* cycle. Out of the attention I have given to the work of Shakespearean theater, thinking especially here of its self-revelations in *Antony and Cleopatra* and in *The Winter's Tale*, I focus on Brünnhilde's thinking to overcome her displacement as bride—a focus rather counter to what I know of the recent valuable studies of Brünnhilde represented, for example, by Carolyn Abbate in her *Unsung Voices*. I take Brünnhilde's actions in the concluding moments of the cycle as a black, or red, wedding ceremony, one to end all weddings. Such an identification or recounting of marriage is how I have proposed understanding the miracle-filled concluding events of Hermione's magic return to life at the end of *Winter's Tale* and Cleopatra's ascension at the end of her play, so that I am in effect taking Brünnhilde's final words, "Siegfried, your wife greets you in joy" *(Selig grüsst dich dein Weib)* as on a par with Cleopatra's "Husband, I come." Both are defiant judgments of the world, but whereas Cleopatra honors the idea of marriage by showing that Antony inspires her to marry transgressively within herself all the roles of women (mother, actress, lover, wife, nurse, queen), Brünnhilde honors its idea by undoing its features, removing her husband's ring and throwing it back to its origins, to culture's origins, those of opera, of music, of marriage, let alone of gold as money; trading the ring back for the horse she had given Siegfried in return for it. That horse, Grane, we were given to understand as representing Brünnhilde's freedom when Wotan, in punishment for her protection of Sieglinde and her child Siegfried, debarred Brünnhilde from riding through the air with her sister Valkyries and condemned her to the obedience of the domestic hearth. Famously invoking Sieglinde's motif sung in praise just once, to Brünnhilde alone, longer than a long opera ago, Brünnhilde now in effect identifies herself with, and as, her husband's mother, and mounts Grane to ride into the flames, as if this unheard-of suttee transfigures a faithfulness to the funeral pyre into the faithful annealing of the wedding. In affirming the incestuous preparation of marriage, Brünnhilde claims marriage without a ring, without forgoing freedom, which will undo the present constructions of the world.

So the undoing suffered by women turns out, as one should have expected, to refer at the same time to the undoing women do. Hence I understand Clément to be claiming it for her writing, which therefore calls for a step toward the end of a world in which steps of change are so disproportionately costly.

Last, I come to Debussy's *Pélleas and Mélisande,* for various reasons anchoring my discussions of instances of women in opera thinking of marriage, or finding it unthinkable. A relatively impersonal reason is the following. If we may construe Wagner's aspiration to a total art work not so much as an idea of the universal encounter of the arts but as one of opera's progressive discovery of its particular powers and conditions as an individual art, thus receiving inspiration and decisively returning inspiration to homologous issues of identity in the other arts; and if this may be understood as an intuition that the medium of opera is known only so far as its definitive instances make it known; then Debussy may be understood as Wagner's principal successor in defining the medium of opera. A permanent argument is engaged between them as to the subject of opera, specifically as to the source of human transcendence as such a subject, whether it is or is not to be thought of as a step within the human. A relatively autobiographical reason is that my introduction to *Pélleas* came in that same summer class with Ernest Bloch, when Bloch would sometimes fall into reminiscences of his time as a music student in Paris at the turn of the century, for example, of going in 1902 to see, with his conservatory companions, the original production of *Pélleas*, which so captivated their sensibilities.

The element that I think has recurred in sudden catches of memory every year since then is Bloch's parody of Debussy's mode of recitative, something he reported that he and his fellow students would invent by the hour, the discovery of an unbroken ethereality into which to set unending banalities. A favorite time for this, naturally, was at dinner, where such utterances as "Please pass the salt," "Thank you," "It's nothing" would take on oceanic waves and calms. Hard to please by contemporary society, Bloch seemed to recapture the early, admiring hilarity as he improvised such instances for us. Only decades later did I learn that parodying this opera was quite characteristic of a sophisticated response to what was quickly recognized as a breakthrough masterpiece of twentieth-century French culture. Proust, no less, composed a well-known *Pélleas* parody (cited in Debussy and Maeterlinck, *Claude Debussy, "Pélleas et Mélisande"*).

Can we understand this impulse? Was this just a late expression of a certain form of theater's always existing on the edge of the ridiculous? Late Shakespeare, again, centers this fact in its study of theater, daring us—freeing us—to withdraw our interest in its events, and our free ratification of them, if we will—in Hermione's statue, after all, despite all, living; in Cleopatra's manic, antic preparations to join her Antony— as if the cloak of conviction is reversed and we are shown the workings that seam together the sublime with the ridiculous. Daring us means again: judge it ridiculous if you're prepared to be judged so, a dare that can be debased, institutionalized, politicized. But opera itself, distinctly, I mean perhaps more characteristically than any other great art, courts the ridiculous—at least more than any before the advent of modern painting and the new music came to dwell with outrage and the threat of fraudulence, exposing judgment as such. Anyone is apt at some time to regard the whole contract of agreeing to take singing for speaking, and to take these inhumanly developed vocal aerialists for persons of exemplary passion, as absurd.

What could be more familiar?—as the sublime Marx Brothers' *A Night at the Opera* exemplarily attests. But also complicates. We are warned of intellectual complication in Groucho's opening line, as he rises from an intimate dinner for two in a swanky restaurant, stares at the check, shouts out, "Nine dollars? Why this is an outrage!" flings the check at his still-seated, alarmed companion and says, "I wouldn't pay it if I were you," and turns on his earthly heel. Now of course the virtuoso outrage is precisely and remorselessly his saying and doing just those things just there—including the truth of them—and we wouldn't not pay its price for the world.

Suppose we ask, Why in this democratic burlesquing of high culture in the instance of opera—farcing or troping the music of "Take Me out to the Ball Game" into the opera's Overture—does this Marx Brothers' film light on *Trovatore* as opera's representative instance? Well, of course, in part for the very reason that everyone lights on it as representative. The commonplace evaluation of the piece, I suppose meant in part to account for its popularity, is that it consists of a sequence of memorable tunes strung on a plot line that is beyond summary and is best ignored. (Its absurdity was featured the last time I heard a celebrity introduce the multitudes to an excellent televised production of the opera.) But my question is, What does the incorporation of just this work elicit in the work of the Marx Brothers?

Before all, I guess, it calls for the attempt of film, one of this species, in finding its happy ending, to find a happy ending for the opera, to transform the guts of imminent ludicrousness into the belly-laugh at the clown's arrival. But why here? Consider that the Marx Brothers sometimes play on the depth of the fact that they are brothers—in one of their greatest routines, in *Duck Soup,* Groucho and Harpo mime each other in synchrony on either side of an arched doorway which they thus establish as a mirror; and in any of their routines Groucho and Chico are absolutely attuned to Harpo's lack of socialization, his infancy (as if he is without speech—Latin in-fans, not yet speaking—because he has successfully refused to subject himself to the confines of grammar, the modification, hence prolongation, of desire), and though Harpo is accordingly incomprehensible to the general, or say the exogamous, the brothers know what he means, or wants, or will accept, without the detours of understanding; to their ears it is heavenly—and devilish—music, as it perhaps is to ours. (Music, like infancy, marks the permanence of the place of understanding as *before* what we might call meaning, as if it exists in permanent anticipation of—hence in perpetual dissatisfaction with, even disdain for—what can be said.) Then if we further consider that *Trovatore* is a story of the repeated substitution of brothers, the film solves the opera's problem by framing it with an end in which the film brothers arrange for the substitution of the right singer to sing in the opera. I take the ecstatic absurdities of their arrangements to be an homage to opera, as a grand opponent, hence a scourge of the so-called absurdities of the arrangements in *Trovatore* that lead to general anguish—their works of absurdity proposing a cathartic freedom from the dark minds, the fixed hatreds, of that world of scorched song.

For just what is absurd? The separation of mothers and children? The rivalry of brothers? The accusation of women as having disruptive powers? A daughter's revenge for violence done her mother? A consequent fear that she has incorporated the mystery, say of revenge, that brought the violence upon her mother? The narrative concentration of such questions on the question of legitimate marriage? This last question is put out of order for the Marx Brothers in their own persons, by the presence of the dowager-figure Margaret Dumont, whose courting by Groucho is a thing too perfect to be touched by further intimacies, if there are any, as befits the relation to a mother. But when there was still a fourth Marx brother, just imaginable as having a romantic interest, and when that interest finds out the wonderful Thelma Todd— as in *Horsefeathers*—then the serious brothers arrange for a final wedding shot in which all three (formally, hence identically, dressed) are lined up alongside the bride and, all three simultaneously undertaking the speech act of the vow and falling together upon their bride for the clinch of finality, tumble with her onto the floor in general felicity. Since the women who in principle share brothers equally are their mothers and their sisters, a certain feature in the wish for marriage is here thrown into discussion.

But the parodic invitation of *Pélleas and Mélisande* trades not on the enjambment of the sublime and the ridiculous but rather on that between the sublime and the ordinary.

Cleopatra's and Brünnhilde's concluding actions are extravagant, out of the ordinary, and meant to be; Mélisande's are on the whole so minimal as almost not to exist, not to originate difference. This may be taken to be her point, to flee without a trace, without evidence of existence, to make no impression. Her first words, famously, are "Ne me touchez pas. Ne me touchez pas." But what is her fear? For whom is she to leave no sign? Such are the questions she elicits from those she encounters in the world she finds herself in. In this opening scene Golaud, her future husband, asks her why she is "so astonished," as if he senses that the world is not her element. She replies, "Are you a giant?"—which recalls for me that in Rousseau's text on the origin of language, in which it is argued that the figurative precedes the literal, Rousseau fantasizes that upon encountering another fellow being for the first time, the impression of fear will produce the name "giant." This fits well enough the sense of our discovering Mélisande at her trauma of discovering for the first time what human beings are capable of. When she goes on to say, "I am lost here. I am not from here. I was not born here," and Golaud replies, "I am lost too," you know she means something like being lost transcendentally, in the world as such; and I think we do not know, though Golaud's reply registers differently, how much he senses a difference in her and how much a similarity with her. Put this as our being doubtful what the difference is, and whether there is any, between the ordinary world and another intervening. But then according to the idea that a condition of opera's singing is the awareness of the doubleness of the world, wouldn't it follow that in setting Maeterlinck's play Debussy is in effect questioning a certain basis of opera? Well, yes.

It is well known that cadences into definite tonalities are as avoided in this music of Debussy as in Wagner's late chromaticism. Another of my music teachers from Berkeley undergraduate days—an accomplished American composer who as a student in the early 1930's had won a prize allowing him to spend two years studying composition in Paris, and who would also describe moments of that time, for example attending the premiere of Stravinsky's Symphony of Psalms, but in such a way that it seemed frighteningly clear to me that he had taken the perfection of that time not to bless his future but to dim it by comparison; it is the terrible risk of the birth of culture in oneself—this musician claimed that there was one perfect cadence in *Pélleas*, associated with Golaud, which he took as a signal of this character's banality of spirit. Looking decades later, not very systematically, for this instance, I found perhaps two such. The hint I have taken from this is to see Mélisande as shrinking from the world precisely in its new guise of ordinariness, interpreted as its banality.

Some such idea, cast as the thought that the beauty of art is the only salvation from the ugliness of the world, would not have been unfamiliar to Maeterlinck and to Debussy; but it does not seem to illuminate the events of this opera. Under what circumstances is banality something one can have a horror of, something that—in the atmosphere of *Pélleas* as in the worlds of other operas—makes breathing difficult? One standing interpretation of banality is as philistinism, understood conventionally as the conventionalism of the bourgeoisie. I would hardly deny that Flaubert may be credited with a horror at the ideas received from this dispensation, but his active opposition in the quest for the true word is closer to Violetta's passive withholding of the word love from what the world calls love than to Mélisande's fear of and astonishment at words as such, at there being a world, one that seeks to know her. Emerson's response to conformity is perhaps a kind of horror at the willingness of human beings to have no voice in their words, which for him suggests an unearthly, haunted existence, and he cannot, I think, in his past of America, attribute this primarily to social and political conditions, or primarily to an individual willingness not to exist. It is as if the cost of the labor of existence had inexplicably risen. The trades of ideas in the air, whose pressure, as Emerson pictures in it "Fate," our words, to be ours, to preserve us, must in every breath oppose (in what he calls aversive thinking), pose a risk of suffocation more like Mélisande's. (Something like this sense of suffocation by a plagiarized world, trading in stolen voices, as if haunted by any claim of originality, is associated with Antonin Artaud's writing in Derrida's "La Parole soufflée," a reading of that writing. I notice its connection with Emerson's "Fate" in the concluding pages of "Notes on the Opening of Wittgenstein's *Investigations*.")

If Wagner may be said to find that his vision of a totality of significance depends on lifting the human beyond itself, Debussy may be said to reverse Wagner in seeking a comparably perpetual transcendence of the human world as internal to the days and nights of that world. (I wish I could better epitomize Vladimir Jankelevitch's marvelous writing about Debussy, in which the concept of geotropism proposes a plane or planet of life for the variations of downward turns in this music—"Ne me touchez pas. Ne me touchez pas"—together with its contrasting phototropisms, let's call them, and with its wavering, trilling, repetitive gestures of stasis.) The question of our relation to the world—whether we are to take a skeptical or a metaphysical attitude toward it, or perhaps to enter again into our neutrality, has here worked itself into a question of atmosphere, a medium of dictatorial mood. Debussy's contemporaries, I gather, perceived his mood as sadness; Emerson recorded an earlier version of the mood with a similar word as if translated from French, chagrin ("Every word they say chagrins us"). Emerson's universalizing of the effect suggests a melancholy lined with vexation, moved this way and that by imperceptible gravities, by unsatisfactory vogues and crowds. Anyone who has heard Mallarmé's description of Maeterlinck's play, in a review written near the time Debussy was deciding to set it, as "musical in the real sense" (as cited in Chapter 4 of Debussy, *Pélleas et Mélisande*, ed. Nichols and Smith) is bound to have a guess at what he had in mind. My guess is that he saw in the play its texture of totality yet discreteness of juxtaposition, of irresolution without indecisiveness, very near to and very far from the resonance of our world, always and never over. It is how I see Debussy's perception of the play's possibilities, as providing a human scale for his own intersections of the sensuous and the abstract, the evanescent and the permanent, assertion without the continuities of assertion, significance without consequence, reference without truth, understanding—as music is supposed to provide understanding—without meaning, the complete awaiting completion, the before and the after of saying. Is this calling upon presence, or letting it go? Perhaps one may speak of it as impressionism. (I am encouraged by Michael Fried's recent series of remarkable essays on writing of the 1890's, in which he reconceives what he is prepared to call impressionism, to regard that discussion as open. The topic will return briefly here.)

The philosophical struggle to take the measure of this clouded human spirit and to recount it should be traced through Rousseau's vision of us as self-imprisoned creatures of freedom, and Wordsworth's of our self-paralyzing withdrawal of interest from the world (sometimes read as boredom, sometimes known as depression), and through Emerson's chronically ridiculed discovery of the mortal need for cheer, confirmed in Nietzsche's combatting of Schopenhauer's call for surcease and in Nietzsche's announcement of the spectre of nihilism. It is an announcement so audible in Heidegger's work that he has specifically to warn (for instance, in *What Is Called Thinking?*) against taking him to be combatting a hopeless pessimism (as in Spengler) with a hopeless optimism (as perhaps in modern science and its organization). And, I have to say, I trace the struggle in Freud's proposal of the death instinct beyond the pleasure principle.

Mélisande's difference from Emerson then becomes crucial. In *This New Yet Unapproachable America* I describe Emerson's monumental essay "Experience" as taking for one of its starting points the classical empiricist's interpretation of experience as made up of impressions and the ideas derived from impressions, and as wishing to "show, in these terms, . . . that, for all our empiricism, nothing (now) makes an impression on us, that we accordingly have no experience (of our own), that we are inexperienced" (p. 92). Then in these terms Mélisande is in the reverse position, in which knowledge and the orientation of thought, as if through some trauma, calling up, say, hysteria, has given to all things an excess and diffusion of impressions, differentiated at their best as waves of the wind, or successions of clouds, or regions of fog or steam or mist, or as lights reflecting on shivering water. (Not accidentally, apparently, has Emerson's prose, from the beginning, as often as it was denied philosophicality, been found to be a mist, sometimes conceded to be golden.) At its worst, or in itself, this excess, I believe, is imagined by philosophers in William James's casual, but endlessly cited, phrase "blooming, buzzing confusion," which seems to me, perhaps because of the repetitive citations, too genteel in its suggestion that there is something prior to language that needs an operation of clarification. I take it we are talking about chaos, to which not clarification is to be brought, but creation.

There is nothing for Mélisande to tell, and she is hence stifled, not because her experience may seem too rare to express, as in the cases of Verdi's Leonora and Violetta in their respective suffocations; but because it is too common for its notation to count as informing anyone of anything. Others, in similar straits, may try making an exception of themselves—not to say a spectacle—by confessing something publicly, hence something that is to be taken as exceptional, such as the fact that they exist, as in Edgar Allan Poe (a favorite of Maeterlinck's): "I felt a maddening desire to shriek aloud. . . . Alas! I well, too well understood that to *think*, in my situation, was to be lost. . . . I bounded like a madman through the crowded thoroughfare. At length, the populous took the alarm, and pursued me" ("The Imp of the Perverse," as quoted in my "Being Odd, Getting Even," p. 123). (The empiricists' picture of the human mind, as formed by impressionistically based ideas, was famously figured by Locke as a tabula rasa, an erased slate. The rationalist reply, as in Leibniz, is that what is in the mind before the onset of impressions, is the (form of the) mind. I believe these pictures continue their life today. In the figure of Mélisande, as in Emerson, both pictures are left behind; the mind can no longer clear itself. In Freud's image in "A Note upon the Mystic Writing-Pad," the detachable, unfrayable surface has come to cleave to its base, as if there is neither past nor future, nothing but unreadable presence and endlessness. Michael Fried's perception of writers like Stephen Crane and Joseph Conrad, incessantly refiguring the appearance of writing on a clean page, is as of one in struggle with the mind as an unerasable slate. If so, something traumatic had happened in the half century since Thoreau's confidence in his variousness with recounting writing (as with a stick in the sand, a hoe in a field, an axe to dismantle and reuse the material of a shack for sharper edification)—unless that confidence was altogether exceptional, then and now, demanding the pair of convictions that one's unintelligibility is not of one's own doing, and that it will not be one's undoing.)

Now Mélisande is evidently past—perhaps just past—Poe's maddening desire to shriek aloud and be pursued by an alarmed populace. She is discovered having already, as she declares, fled—only to discover that she is, in an obsessive image of Poe's, immured, but within the world. On Michelet's testimony, in steeping oneself in Registers of the Inquisitions of the fourteenth century, "what especially strikes one is not merely the vast numbers of those punished, but the multitude of persons *immured*, shut up, that is to say, in a tiny stone cell, or in a dungeon. . . . Women died of the terror of being walled up in the little black hole" (pp. 312, 314). An experience, told unforgettably, from the side of its victim, as simultaneously and wherever you are one of fleeing and of being immured—no wonder Clément takes Michelet as one of hers.

My insistence on this experience of Debussy's opera as one in which thinking is, so to speak, ontologically disbarred places thinking in a world of absolute unoriginality, in which, since nothing originates in any soul, there is nothing but suffering, however much vexed motion there may be in such a world. It is a world of absolute philistinism (the common theme of Nietzsche's *Untimely Meditations*, one of which, titularly on Schopenhauer, is so critical in the course of Emersonian perfectionism), not obviously attributable to any particular class or any particular political orientation, terrified by change, petrified by unchange, as if making explicit that Nietzsche's characterization of nihilism as a revenge against time's "It was" is at the same time a revenge against the foreseeable future. Here is the urgency of Emerson's call for the new, which is to say, of his discovery that the new world remains undiscovered, half a step away, and behind us. And of course nothing more risks philistinism than forever canting and catching up to the sundry new. Between this urgency and this risk is how I place that ancient shock or strain of philosophy, shared in by positivist and by deconstructionist sensibilities, upon coming to itself in the cave of the ordinary—the ordinary, hence, as conformity, banality, rigidity, illusion; Wittgenstein will in addition specify lostness, distraction, perverseness, disappointment. The strain is caught in the parodical or parodiable distance between Mélisande's flight from the ordinary and Debussy's recounting of it. The irony of this distance—though I doubt that I have the means to show it—is that it is not ironic.

Since after the failures in America's self-discovery, and after the successes in Europe's self-destruction, there is—with perhaps one exception—no place *else* for Western thinking to be—and no words *else* to say, if there is to be anything new it must evidently be prepared by a new understanding of what is else, hence of what else understanding and discovery can be. (The exception I leave open is what is called Israel. The price of taking it as an alternative is of making it one place among others. I do not yet trust myself to do this, or not to.)

Now I close by once more questioning my credentials in supposing that these notes, whose intervals have begun running quite out of hand, are mine to strike. As earnest, I append two further notes, one historical, the other as it were philosophical.

First history. Maurice Maeterlinck, of all people, forms a notable linking in American culture's conversation with itself, or failure of it. That he was an admirer of Emerson's writing is not exactly news these days (though until recently either it was new to me, or I had forgotten it through having no use for the knowledge), yet how deep his admiration was may still be surprising to hear. That John Dewey was in turn an admirer of Maeterlinck is more likely to be unfamiliar, and initially to be even less plausible. In a sense it seemed implausible to Dewey, if we go by his 1911 review-essay of, I gather, Maeterlinck's *On Emerson and Other Essays*. He finds central sentiments and ideas of his own so well formulated in Maeterlinck's words (on topics pertaining to nothing less than what Dewey calls the present barrenness of philosophy) that he quotes them at length to this effect; yet Dewey declares himself incompetent to paraphrase Maeterlinck's prose. What's the matter? Without trying now to verify it, it strikes me—since Dewey quotes an encomium of Maeterlinck's among many in his essay on Emerson, and expresses gratitude for it; and since I have to assume, from Dewey's own fervent essay on Emerson, that he recognizes the extraordinary paraphrasing of Emerson in Maeterlinck's prose—that the figure Dewey is more significantly confessing his inability to paraphrase is Emerson, the one whose writing he misses in his own, whose words he cannot bury in his own. This matters to me in being at odds with the common view—perhaps it is the price—of the recent revival of interest in Emerson, I believe not just in North America, which takes Emerson as, let's say, a proto-pragmatist. This from my perspective serves to continue the repression of Emerson's words which has shaped his reception.

Here is a sample of three sentences of Maeterlinck on Emerson (identified by the translator of the book in question in his Foreword to it as Maeterlinck's "avowed master and greatest influence"): "He is nearer than any other to our common life. He is the most attentive, the most assiduous, the most honest, the most scrupulous, and probably the most human of guides. He is the sage of commonplace days, and commonplace days are in sum the substance of our being." This is of course congenial to my sense of Emerson (and Thoreau) as underwriting ordinary language philosophy. But the incessant Emersonian turns of thought in Maeterlinck will prove as hard to remember as it has been to credit Nietzsche's strumming of Emersonian transfigurations.

What remains constant, yet to be understood, is the virtual impossibility of keeping handy a serious view of Emerson. I do not say that it is as important to listen for Emerson in the case of Maeterlinck as in that of Nietzsche, yet the connection with Debussy and his Mélisande is grand.

Does this bit of history answer, or does it raise further, the question of my right to a say in the region of opera? Catherine Clément reports something to ponder about where the say can come from. "Opera comes to me from the womb. . . . They will tell you that hysteria is a sickness. . . . Do not believe it. Hysteria is woman's principal resource" (p. 176). The stakes in play for me are marked in Clément's going on to say, or sing, that "the uterus, which is where hysteria comes from, is an organ where the thought of beings is conceived," which pretty much identifies skepticism with respect to other minds as a male affair. She acknowledges exceptions. She names in this passage, as having seen, in flashes, the way of thinking peculiar to women, Michelet, Diderot, and Freud. Who knows what others there must be? Clément could have mentioned, perhaps it goes without saying, Nietzsche, in such a passage as the following from *The Birth of Tragedy* (§21):

> I must not appeal to those who use the images of what happens on the stage, the words and emotions of the acting persons, in order to approach with their help the musical feeling; for these people do not speak music as their mother tongue and, in spite of this help, never get beyond the entrance halls of musical perception. . . . I must appeal only to those who, immediately related to music, have in it, as it were, their motherly womb, and are related to things almost exclusively through unconscious musical relations.

Am I ready to vow, as when Bloch asked us whether we heard through to Bach, that I have the ear, that I know my mother's mother tongue of music to be also mine? The hills are different ones now, but the world is, I'm glad to say, the same when I have to catch my breath at such promises. Are they mine? Have I, throughout these pages, been asking anything else?

~ Bibliography

Abbate, Carolyn. *Unsung Voices: Opera and Musical Narrative in the Nineteenth Century.* Princeton: Princeton University Press, 1991.

Aristophanes. *The Clouds,* trans. William Arrowsmith. In *The Complete Greek Comedy,* ed. William Arrowsmith. Ann Arbor: University of Michigan Press, 1962.

———*The Frogs,* trans. Richard Lattimore. In *The Complete Greek Comedy,* ed. William Arrowsmith. Ann Arbor: University of Michigan Press, 1962.

Artaud, Antonin. *Antonin Artaud: Selected Writings.* New York: Farrar, Straus and Giroux, 1976.

Augustine. *The Confessions of St. Augustine,* trans. E. B. Pusey, foreword by A. H. Armstrong. New York: Dutton, 1970.

Austin, J. L. *How to Do Things with Words,* 2nd ed., ed. J. O. Urmsom and Marina Sbisa. Cambridge, Mass.: Harvard University Press, 1975.

———"Other Minds." In *Philosophical Papers.*

———*Philosophical Papers,* 3rd ed., ed. J. O. Urmsom and G. J. Warnock. Oxford: Oxford University Press, 1962.

———"A Plea for Excuses." In *Philosophical Papers.*

———"Pretending." In *Philosophical Papers.*

———*Sense and Sensibilia,* reconstructed from the manuscript notes by G. J. Warnock. Oxford: Oxford University Press, 1962.

Ayer, Alfred Jules. *The Foundations of Empirical Knowledge.* London: St. Martin's Press, 1955.

———*Language, Truth, and Logic.* New York: Dover, 1952.

Beckett, Samuel. *Endgame.* New York: Grove Press, 1958.

Berkeley, George. *A Treatise Concerning the Principles of Human Knowledge.* London: J. M. Dent & Sons, 1950.

Bishop, Elizabeth. "Visits to St. Elizabeths." In *Elizabeth Bishop: The Complete Poems.* New York: Farrar, Straus, and Giroux, 1969.

Bizet, Georges. *Georges Bizet, "Carmen": English National Opera Guide 13* (libretto and introductory articles), ed. Nicholas John. New York: Riverrun Press, 1982.

Cavell, Stanley. "The Availability of Wittgenstein's Later Philosophy." In *Must We Mean What We Say?*.

————"The Avoidance of Love: A Reading of *King Lear*." In *Disowning Knowledge*.

————"Being Odd, Getting Even." In *In Quest of the Ordinary: Lines of Skepticism and Romanticism*. Chicago: University of Chicago Press, 1988.

————*The Claim of Reason: Wittgenstein, Skepticism, Morality, and Tragedy*. Oxford: Oxford University Press, 1979.

————*Conditions Handsome and Unhandsome*. Chicago: University of Chicago Press, 1990.

————*Disowning Knowledge*. Cambridge: Cambridge University Press, 1987.

————"Ending the Waiting Game." In *Must We Mean What We Say?*

————"Hamlet's Burden of Proof." In *Disowning Knowledge*.

————"Kierkegaard's *On Authority and Revelation*." In *Must We Mean What We Say?*

————"Knowing and Acknowledging." In *Must We Mean What We Say?*

————*Must We Mean What We Say? A Book of Essays*. Cambridge: Cambridge University Press, 1976.

————"Must We Mean What We Say?" In *Must We Mean What We Say?*

————"Notes on the Opening of Wittgenstein's *Investigations*." Forthcoming in 1994 from Basil Blackwell in *Cavell Thinking*.

————"The Politics of Interpretation." In *Themes out of School: Effects and Causes*. Chicago: University of Chicago Press, 1988.

————"Postscript (1989)." *Critical Inquiry,* Winter 1990.

————*Pursuits of Happiness: The Hollywood Comedy of Remarriage*. Cambridge, Mass.: Harvard University Press, 1981.

————"Psychoanalysis and Cinema: The Melodrama of the Unknown Woman." In *The Trial(s) of Psychoanalysis*, ed. Francoise Meltzer. Chicago: University of Chicago Press, 1988.

————*The Senses of Walden*. San Francisco: North Point Press, 1981.

————*This New Yet Unapproachable America: Lectures after Emerson after Wittgenstein*. Albuquerque: Living Batch Press, 1989.

————*The World Viewed*. Cambridge, Mass.: Harvard University Press, 1979.

Clément, Catherine. *The Lives and Legends of Jacques Lacan*, trans. Arthur Goldhammer. New York: Columbia University Press, 1983.

————*Opera, or the Undoing of Women*, trans. Betsy Wing with a foreword by Susan McClary. Minneapolis: University of Minnesota Press, 1988.

Conant, James. "Must We Show What We Cannot Say." In *The Senses of Stanley Cavell*, ed. Richard Fleming and Michael Payne. Lewisburg, Penn.: Bucknell University Press, 1989.

————"The Search for Logically Alien Thought: Descartes, Kant, Frege, and the *Tractatus*." *Philosophical Topics*, 20, no. 1 (Fall 1991).

Debussy, Claude. *Claude Debussy, "Pelléas et Mélisande,"* ed. Roger Nichols and Richard Langham Smith. Cambridge: Cambridge University Press, 1989.

Debussy, Claude, and Maeterlinck, Maurice. *Claude Debussy, "Pelléas et Mélisande": English National Opera Guide, 9* (libretto and introductory articles). New York: Riverrun Press, 1982.

Derrida, Jacques. *Glas*, trans. John P. Leavey Jr. and Richard Rand. Lincoln: University of Nebraska Press, 1986.

————*Of Grammatology*, trans. Gayatri Chakravorty Spivak. Baltimore: John Hopkins University Press, 1976.

————*Otobiographies: L'enseignement de Nietzsche et la politique du nom propre*. Paris: Editions Galilée, 1984. (Translated with the exception of part I, "Declarations d'Indépendance," together with roundtable discussions in *The Ear of the Other*, trans. Peggy Kamuf, ed. Christie V. MacDonald; New York: Schocken Books, 1985.)

————"La Parole soufflée." In *Writing and Difference*, trans. Alan Bass. Chicago: University of Chicago Press, 1978.

————"Signature Event Context." In *Limited Inc.*, ed. Gerald Graff. Evanston: Northwestern University Press, 1988. (Derrida's original essay, his reply to Searle, and a new response are printed together in *Limited Inc*. Searle's response in *Glyph I* to Derrida's original essay is not reprinted.)

————*Speech and Phenomena: And Other Essays on Husserl's Theory of Signs*, trans. with an introduction by David B. Allison, preface by Newton Garver. Evanston: Northwestern University Press, 1973.

Descartes, René. *Meditations*, ed. Laurence J. Lafleur. Indianapolis: Bobbs-Merrill, 1951.

Dewey, John. "Emerson—The Philosopher of Democracy." In *Middle Works*, vol. 3, *Essays on the New Empiricism*.

————"Maeterlinck's Philosophy of Life." In *Middle Works*, vol. 6, *How We Think and Selected Essays*.

————*Middle Works, 1899–1924*, 15 vols., ed. Jo Ann Boydston with an introduction by Joe R. Burnett. Carbondale: Southern Illinois University Press, 1985.

Emerson, Ralph Waldo. "The American Scholar." In *Selections from Ralph Waldo Emerson*.

———"Circles." In *Essays and Lectures*.

———"Considerations by the Way." In *The Conduct of Life* in *Essays and Lectures*.

———*Essays and Lectures*, ed. Joel Porte. New York: Library of America, 1983.

———"Experience." In *Selections from Ralph Waldo Emerson*.

———"Fate." In *Essays and Lectures*.

———*Selections from Ralph Waldo Emerson*, ed. Stephen E. Whicher. Boston: Houghton Mifflin, 1957.

———"Self-Reliance." In *Selections from Ralph Waldo Emerson*.

Euripides. *Hyppolytus*, trans. David Grene in *Euripides I*, with an introduction by Richard Lattimore, in *The Complete Greek Tragedies*, ed. David Grene and Richard Lattimore. Chicago: University of Chicago Press, 1955.

Felman, Shoshana. *The Literary Speech Act: Don Juan with J. L. Austin, or Seduction in Two Languages*, trans. Catherine Porter. Ithaca: Cornell University Press, 1983.

Frege, Gottlob. *The Foundations of Arithmetic: A Logico-Mathematical Enquiry into the Concept of a Number*, 2nd rev. ed., trans. J. L. Austin. Evanston: Northwestern University Press, 1980.

———"Logic" (I). In *Posthumous Writings*, ed. Hans Hermes, Friedrich Kambartel, and Friedrich Kaulbach, trans. Peter Long and Roger White. Chicago: University of Chicago Press, 1979.

———"On Sense and Reference," trans. Max Black. In *Translations from the Philosophical Writings of Gottlob Frege*, ed. Peter Geach and Max Black. Oxford: Basil Blackwell, 1952. (Reprinted as "On Sense and Meaning" in *Collected Papers on Mathematics, Logic, and Philosophy*, ed. Brian McGuinness, trans. Max Black, V. H. Dudman, Peter Geach, Hans Kaal, E. H. W. Kluge, Brian McGuinness, and R. H. Stoothoff; Oxford: Basil Blackwell, 1984.)

Freud, Sigmund. *Civilization and Its Discontents*. In *Standard Edition*, vol. 21.

———*Fragment of an Analysis of a Case of Hysteria* (Dora) (1905). In *Standard Edition*, vol. 7.

———*On Narcissism: An Introduction* (1914). In *Standard Edition*, vol. 14.

———"A Note upon the Mystic Writing-Pad" (1900). In *Standard Edition*, vol. 19.

———"Negation" (1925). In *Standard Edition*, vol. 19.

————The Standard Edition of the Complete Psychological Works of Sigmund Freud, 24 vols., ed. and trans. James Strachey in collaboration with Anna Freud. London: Hogarth Press, 1953.

Fried, Michael. "Almayer's Face: On 'Impressionism' in Conrad, Crane and Norris." Criticial Inquiry, Winter 1992.

————"Stephen Crane's Upturned Faces." In Realism, Writing, Disfiguration: On Thomas Eakins and Stephen Crane. Chicago: University of Chicago Press, 1987.

Friedlander, Eli. "Expressions of Judgment." Ph.D. diss., Harvard University, 1992.

Frye, Northrop. A Natural Perspective. New York: Columbia University Press, 1965.

Heidegger, Martin. Being and Time, trans. J. Macquarrie and E. Robinson. New York: Harper Books, 1962.

————"The Origin of the Work of Art." In Poetry, Language, Thought, trans. Albert Hofstadter. New York: Harper and Row, 1968.

————What Is Called Thinking? trans. J. Glenn Gray. New York: Harper and Row, 1971.

Hill, Geoffrey. The Lords of Limit. London: Deutsch, 1984.

James, Henry. "The Beast in the Jungle." In Great Short Works of Henry James. New York: Harper and Row, 1966.

Jankelevitch, Vladimir. Debussy et le mystère de l'instant. Paris: Plon, 1876.

Kant, Immanuel. The Critique of Pure Reason, trans. Norman Kemp Smith. New York: St. Martin's Press, 1965.

————Foundations of the Metaphysics of Morals, trans. and with an introduction by Lewis White Beck. Indianapolis: Bobbs-Merrill, 1978.

Kerman, Joseph. Opera as Drama. Berkeley: University of California Press, 1988.

Klein, Melanie. The Psychoanalysis of Children. London: Hogarth, 1982.

Koestenbaum, Wayne. The Queen's Throat: Opera, Homosexuality, and the Mystery of Desire. New York: Poseidon Press, 1993.

Kripke, Saul. Wittgenstein on Rules and Private Language. Cambridge: Cambridge University Press, 1982.

Kristeva, Julia. Tales of Love, trans. Leon S. Roudiez. New York: Columbia University Press, 1987.

Lacan, Jacques. "Ego-Ideal and the Ideal Ego." In The Seminar of Jacques Lacan.

————"The Fluctuations of the Libido." In The Seminar of Jacques Lacan.

————"On Narcissism" and "The Two Narcissisms." In The Seminar of Jacques Lacan.

————The Seminar of Jacques Lacan: Book I, Freud's Paper on Technique, 1953–

1954, ed. Jacques-Alain Miller, trans. with notes by John Forrester. New York: W. W. Norton, 1975.

Laplanche, Jean, and J. B. Pontalis. "Fantasy and the Origins of Sexuality." *International Journal of Psychoanalysis*, 1968. (Translated from *Les Temps Modernes*, April 1964.)

Levinas, Emmanuel. "Transcendence as the Idea of Infinity." In *Totality and Infinity*. Pittsburgh: Duquesne University Press, 1969.

———"Philosophy and the Idea of Infinity." In *Collected Philosophical Papers*. Dordrecht: Martinus Nijhoff, 1987.

Lewis, Clarence Irving. *Mind and the World Order*. New York: Dover, 1956.

Locke, John. *An Essay Concerning Human Understanding*, ed. with an introduction by P. H. Nidditch. Oxford: Clarendon Press, 1975.

Maeterlinck, Maurice. *On Emerson and Other Essays*, trans. Montrose J. Moses. Great Neck, N.Y.: Roth Publishing, 1978.

Malcolm, Norman. "The Privacy of Experience." In *Thought and Knowledge*. Ithaca: Cornell University Press, 1977.

Michelet, Jules. *Satanism and Witchcraft*, trans. A. R. Allinson. New York: Citadel Press, 1939.

Mill, John Stuart. *On the Subjection of Women*, with an introduction by Wendell Robert Carr. Cambridge, Mass.: MIT Press, 1970.

———*On Liberty*, ed. Elizabeth Rapaport. Indianapolis: Hackett, 1987.

Monteverdi, Claudio. *Claudio Monteverdi, "Orfeo,"* ed. John Whenham. Cambridge: Cambridge University Press, 1986. (Monteverdi's alteration of the ending of *Orfeo* is discussed in chapter 2, F. W. Sternfeld's "The Orpheus Myth and the Libretto 'Orfeo.'")

Mozart, Wolfgang Amadeus. *Wolfgang Amadeus Mozart, "The Marriage of Figaro": English National Opera Guide, 17* (libretto and introductory articles), ed. Nicholas John. New York: Riverrun Press, 1983.

Nietzsche, Friedrich. *"The Birth of Tragedy" and "The Case of Wagner,"* trans. with commentary by Walter Kaufmann. New York: Vintage Books, 1967.

———*Ecce Homo*, trans. Walter Kaufmann and R. J. Hollingdale. New York: Vintage Books, 1967.

———*Schopenhauer as Educator*. In *Untimely Meditations*, trans. R. J. Hollingdale with an introduction by J. P. Stern. Cambridge: Cambridge University Press, 1983.

———*Thus Spoke Zarathustra*, trans. Walter Kaufmann. New York: Penguin Books, 1978.

———"Why I Write Such Excellent Books." In *Ecce Homo*.

Ovid. *Metamorphoses,* trans. A. D. Melville with an introduction and notes by E. J. Kenney. Oxford: Oxford University Press, 1966.

Plato. *The Republic,* trans. G. M. A. Grube. Indianapolis: Hackett, 1974.

———*Symposium,* trans. Michael Joyce in *The Dialogues of Plato,* ed. Edith Hamilton and Huntington Cairns. New York: Pantheon Books, 1961.

Poe, Edgar Allan. *Collected Works,* 3 vols, ed. Thomas Ollive Mabbot. Cambridge, Mass.: Harvard University Press, 1978.

———"The Imp of the Perverse." In *Collected Works,* vol. 3.

———"The Purloined Letter." In *Collected Works,* vol. 3.

Ricks, Christopher. "Austin's Swink." *University of Toronto Quarterly,* 61, no. 3 (Spring 1992).

Rousseau, Jean-Jacques. *On the Origin of Language,* trans. with an afterword by John H. Moran and Alexander Gode, with an introduction by Alexander Gode. Chicago: University of Chicago Press, 1966.

———*On the Social Contract,* trans. Judith R. Masters and ed. Roy D. Masters. New York: St. Martin's Press, 1978.

Scholem, Gershom. "Walter Benjamin and His Angel." In *On Jews and Judaism in Crisis: Selected Essays,* ed. Werner J. Dannhauser. New York: Schocken Books, 1976.

Schopenhauer, Arthur. *The World as Will and Representation,* vol. 1, trans. E. F. J. Payne. Indiana Hills: The Falcon's Wing Press, 1958.

Searle, John R. "Reiterating the Difference: A Reply to Derrida." In *Glyph I,* ed. Samuel Webster and Henry Sussman. Baltimore: Johns Hopkins University Press, 1977.

———*Speech Acts: An Essay in the Philosophy of Language.* London: Cambridge University Press, 1969.

Sedgwick, Eve Kosofsky. "The Beast in the Closet: James and the Writing of Homosexual Panic." In *Sex, Politics, and Science in the Nineteenth-Century Novel,* ed. Ruth Bernard Yeazell. Baltimore: Johns Hopkins University Press, 1986.

Shakespeare, William. *Anthony and Cleopatra,* ed. M. R. Ridley, based on the edition of R. H. Case. Cambridge, Mass.: Harvard University Press, 1956.

———*Coriolanus,* ed. Philip Brockbank. London: Methuen, 1976.

———*Hamlet,* ed. Harold Jenkins. London: Methuen, 1982.

———*King Lear,* ed. Kenneth Muir, based on the edition of W. J. Craig. Cambridge, Mass.: Harvard University Press, 1959.

———*The Merchant of Venice,* ed. John Russell Brown. London: Methuen, 1969.

———*Othello,* ed. M. R. Ridley. London: Methuen, 1964.

———*The Winter's Tale*, ed. J. H. P. Pafford. Cambridge, Mass.: Harvard University Press, 1963.

Spengler, Oswald. *The Decline of the West*, abridged ed., Modern Library translation. New York: Random House, 1962.

Strawson, P. F. *Individuals: An Essay in Descriptive Metaphysics*. London: Methuen, 1964.

Thoreau, Henry David. *Walden*, annotated by Walter Harding. New York: Washington Square Press, 1963.

Verdi, Guiseppe. *Giuseppe Verdi, "La Traviata": English National Opera Guide*, 5 (libretto and introductory articles), ed. Nicholas John. New York: Riverrun Press, 1981.

———*Giuseppe Verdi, Il Trovatore: English National Opera Guide*, 20 (libretto and introductory articles). New York: Riverrun Press, 1982.

Wagner, Richard. *Götterdämerung*. In *The Authentic Librettos of the Wagner Operas*. New York: Crown, 1938.

Williams, William Carlos. *In the American Grain*, with an introduction by Horace Gregory. New York: New Direction Books, 1956.

Wittgenstein, Ludwig. *Philosophical Investigations*, trans. G. E. M. Anscombe. New York: Macmillan, 1953.

———*Tractatus Logico-Philosophicus*, trans. D. F. Pears and B. F. McGuinness. London: Routledge & Kegan Paul, 1961.

———*Wittgenstein and the Vienna Circle*, conversations recorded by Friedrich Waisman, ed. Brian McGuinness, trans. Joachim Schulte and Brian McGuinness. Oxford: Basil Blackwell, 1979.

Wordsworth, William. "Preface to the Second Edition of *Lyrical Ballads*." In *Selected Poems and Prefaces*, ed. Jack Stillinger. Boston: Houghton Mifflin, 1965.

∿ Acknowledgments

Each of these chapters represents some degree of departure from anything I have so far published, and my requests for the judgment of friends about my early drafts showed matching new degrees of concern. Thanks are, accordingly, due first to Jay Cantor, James Conant, Arnold Davidson, Timothy Gould, John Hollander, William Rothman, and Marc Shell, not alone for their comments on specific passages, but for timely supplies of encouragement. More specific debts, especially in the absence of notes, will take more time.

Early formulations of ideas in the second chapter relating affinities and differences in Austin's and Derrida's hopes for and despair of, or farewells to, philosophy were broached in a seminar at Harvard in 1986 called "The Philosophy of the Ordinary"; these were taken up and elaborated a bit in the summer of 1991 in the seminar I offered at The School of Criticism and Theory at Dartmouth; after the delivery in 1992 of the second Jerusalem lecture incorporating these ideas, compressed versions of what became the second chapter, or excerpts with transitional summaries, were given at Indiana University for the annual meetings of the Association for Comparative Literature in March of 1993, then for a colloquium at Brandeis, and finally on one of a set of productive spring days at Bucknell University. I mention these events because each of them produced remarkably rewarding discussion periods, moments of which reentered and modified the full version presented here. There should be conventions for collecting the names of the many voices I know I profited from. At Indiana there were at least two of the best exchanges I remember having had on such occasions, with people who had vanished when afterward I tried to find them to learn their names. One of them began with the question, given how much more closely I wished to interweave Derrida with Austin than one might have expected, of how I epitomized what it is that Derrida did not want to hear in Austin, which elicited from me the response: that philosophy was an effect of the ordinary. Another was then prompted to ask what Austin did not want to hear that left room for Derrida, which elicited from me: that the ordinary cannot block, but can only inspire, skepticism. But it is the elaboration that matters, and I know I have not done it justice in my final text. After the Brandeis version, William Flesch and Richard Moran raised doubts about the relation between utterances and actions, or utterances as actions, which caused me to expand what I had so far said on the subject. Early, for the seminar on the Ordinary, Nancy Bauer wrote a paper on Derrida's treatment of Austin which produced profitable conversations; late, at Bucknell, as the result of a faculty seminar on a version of that material, Richard Fleming and Michael Payne usefully pressed me on issues relating it, respectively, to Emerson and to Lacan.

It was Steven Affeldt who, in the course of one or another exchange about these chapters, first asked me, almost doubtfully, since the work had come up before, whether in the *Symposium* Plato did not cite the same quotation from Euripides' *Hippolytus* whose citing by Austin I keep coming back to. I was as stunned by having forgotten this as I was by having failed for so long to take the citation seriously in Austin's text. At Bucknell I began elaborating the significance of Austin's accordingly invoking simultaneously the *Hippolytus* and the *Symposium*, beginning with the suggestion that Socrates' closing speculation about the relation of tragedy and comedy was being inscribed; and in an informal group at a reception afterward, Jean Peterson adduced suddenly, and a little hesitantly, *The Frogs*, then disappeared to return a few minutes later with a text of Aristophanes' play, sure enough sporting the same tag. After I reported this, back at Harvard, to Paul Franks, we sensed that Austin was exploiting something that must once have been a commonplace, and Franks some days later produced further occurrences of the Euripides line, once elsewhere in Plato and in two later Roman texts. I dramatize these scenes a little, rather than settling for a list of names for acknowledgment, in order to tap experiences most writers will recognize, and thereby to formulate what should be a familiar question about reading, or rather about not reading: the more my ignorance and inattentiveness sting me in such a matter, along with my gasps of pleasure in overcoming both, the more I ask why those with more pertinent learning or presence of mind than I command had not previously (so far as I know) stopped at Austin's quite astonishing gesture of quoting Euripides' Greek in his apparently otherwise unaccommodating text. Say that it has to do with its simply making no sense that Austin would seriously be invoking tragedy in his airy prose. Then where does the sense of Austin come from against which this makes no sense? (This is a version of my problem with Emerson, against the fixated image of whom, as lacking the tragic sense, it makes no sense to suppose that Nietzsche, the theorist of tragedy, was unendingly and happily indebted. Making no sense, having no use, it is bound to be forgotten, unendingly.)

This is a place to note an important text on Austin's work on performative utterances, Shoshana Felman's *The Literary Speech Act: Don Juan with J. L. Austin, or Seduction in Two Languages*, whose absence of discussion in my text is perhaps its most notable omission. If there is a good excuse for this omission it is that this text deserves a response on its own, and defies positioning within the boundaries, more or less incommensurable with hers, that I have placed or displaced for myself here. I say this because of my guess that the cause of the neglect of Austin's citation from Euripides is a function of underestimating Austin's, let's say, seriousness. Although I believe Shoshana Felman does not mention the Euripides quotation, I do not for an instant sense that the Austin she portrays is incapable of the thought. I am not proud to have to say that I have paused only in the course of these Acknowledgments to finish reading her book; her sense of Austin's play with seriousness, and of the role of tragedy in the act of promising, and contrariwise, is evident. In a sense her featuring of Don Juan assumes an oscillation with tragedy. When I began to read her book, at the time of my 1986 seminar on the ordinary mentioned earlier, the closeness and distance of her sense of things to and from my own seemed to swamp rather than raise topics for discussion. For example, she says early, "To seduce is to produce felicitous language" (p. 28). This is attractive, but shall we be seduced so soon? It seems a direct counter to Austin's way of thinking, yet it seems here to be counting on it. The felicitous in Austin, or rather the infelicitous, is the title of a set of conditions (Austin may say rules) the infringing of any of which is the cause of a performative utterance's failing to do what it has set out to do, for instance, make a promise. But the utterances for which infelicity is thus defined are exactly those which turn out to be illocutionary, not perlocutionary, in force (or logic, or nature?); and since to seduce is archetypically not illocutionary, for Austin it makes no sense to say that the language of seduction either is or is not felicitous. Or is this too sober? You could say the seductive is that which has (is possible only where there are) no rules or conditions; or you could say it is possible only in the infringement of rules; or you could say it improvises its conditions. Perhaps "to seduce is to produce felicitious language" says one or another of these things. But then how is the logic of seduction different from that of wounding or horrifying? (Should we expect it to be?)

As one of the two epigraphs to her preface, Felman cites Nietzsche's superb remark "To breed an animal with the right to make promises . . . is it not man's true problem?" But can we afford to let the difference between making a promise and being promising remain inexplicit? Isn't that what seduction does? I have elsewhere taken that remark of Nietzsche's as suggesting that speaking as such is being identified here as making promises, which is to say, giving one's word. (This suggests that it is speech, which is to say, language, that is what Nietzsche calls man's true problem. Which further suggests that the sense of a promise as something thrown beyond itself, like a word, outlines the concept of "having" a self, no doubt a reason one thinks, dangerously, of the self as a function of "having" language.) Perhaps an identification of speaking as promising, which fairly patly characterizes Don Juan, is Felman's point, which thus proposes rooting language in seduction as opposed to (what Austin calls) the bond. I too have expressed dissatisfaction with Austin's picture there, but a portrait of him that likens him to Don Juan (Felman, p. 122) must not fail to see the depth to which Austin presents himself as a husband and father. I can see taking this to be his most seductive claim, but then the matter comes to formulating the relation of law and infringement, whether in Austin these destroy or reconstitute each other. I beg off further discussion here, one I hope to see taken up in the future, by recalling for the interested reader how variously the issue of the legitimacy of marriage has over the years preoccupied my own thoughts about comedy and tragedy in relation to skepticism.

A further event bearing on the question of the performative deserves mention here. At the English Institute in the summer of 1993, in a panel organized and introduced by Eve Kosofsky Sedgwick under the title "Performance and Performativity," two philosophers—Judith Butler and Timothy Gould—began their contributions, each complex and of great interest, with an account of Austin's work, and both cited Nietzsche, but it was unclear to me in listening how either of these contributions is meant, or can be seen, to face the other. (Here, as anywhere, the rift in the traditions of philosophy may be exacting its duties. I cannot deny it; but who wants to settle for it?) While Gould noted, as uncontentious, that Austin has, perhaps unfortunately, little to say about the perlocutionary force of utterances that is comparable to his articulation of illocutionary force, Butler, focusing on the violence of hate speech and the political violence exerted in suppressing it (that is, denying the absolute "freedom" of speech), dealt with examples that are without exception within the realm of the perlocutionary, anyway beyond the illocutionary. This, as it were, division of labor, alerts me to say that I have not, in the preceding chapters, except implicitly (for example, in denying that excuses apply to utterances as they do to— other—actions), asked what it betokens that human speech is characterized by both forces, that, to use images of Nietzsche, words both bind and wound. It is surely comprehensible that the perlocutionary utterance should be felt to be as paradigmatic of human speech—say, of the fact that saying something is doing something—as the illocutionary utterance is, taken so even in preference to the illocutionary utterance. It is equally, to my mind, unhappy that an understanding of this preference should be sought, or avoided, by slighting Austin's perception of this difference. A corrective to this practice is bound to consider the ample territories tracked by Butler and by Gould.

For me to have gone further than I have in Chapter 2 would have meant going beyond the point at which I claim that Austin's intuitive identification of speaking as sometimes acting comes undone. Austin, for example in "A Plea for Excuses," suggests various lines of investigation that the fact of excuses opens for studying the concept of human action. One, broached in my chapter, is of actions at the limit of excuses, those which require, "instead," apology and reparation. Another is the extent to which what human beings make happen can be grasped in considering their doing things, one after the other, as if human actions came into the world stacked and trimmed rather than webbed and nested. In noting a difference a moment ago between being promising and making promises I have suggested the more general question of how a person's being something (seductive, rejecting, nurturant, haughty, vivid, serious, funny) comes into the judgment of what the person has made happen, or kept from happening. Here the issue of human passiveness, or passion, as the other of human action, may productively enter, a topic that Timothy Gould has importantly urged in several earlier papers dealing with Austin's work. But these are matters that seem to me, or seemed, mostly to go quite beyond my idea in reconsidering Derrida's encounter with Austin, which was for me to take up the illumination of Austin's theory of the performative in its strengths, and to indicate certain of its connections with other regions of his work.

Part of the fortune in having continuing conversations with young friends like James Conant is that, for one instance, when you say to them that you want to go beyond what you had written earlier (in "The Politics of Interpretation") about Frege's bearing on Austin's issue of the seriousness of assertion, but that you have not found a text that quite epitomizes that bearing, they lead you to the passage from Frege quoted in Chapter 2 at pages 95–96.

The material on opera, Chapter 3, is so selective that it is pointless to remark on what is not there. What it is selected from is mostly the work assigned members of a seminar on film and opera that I offered in the spring of 1992, in which I failed to get the philosophers and the musicians to talk to each other. Perhaps the present text will further this goal next time. In Jerusalem, I paused in the middle of that last lecture, before moving to the discussion of illustrative passages from six operas, to play a tape consisting of a juxtaposition of roughly one-minute excerpts from each of the passages. The effect of the music on the audience was electric; it was difficult to want to continue with words afterward. I expressed my sense of the moment by saying that, however selective my remarks, I would be satisfied if, however they might generalize, they met the experience of just those six minutes of opera fragments. For the preparation of that tape I am, we all were, indebted to Eli Friedlander and Michal Grover-Friedlander. Michal Grover-Friedlander is completing a Ph.D. dissertation at Brandeis University on the deaths of women in a number of Verdi's operas. She and I have discussed opera on a number of occasions; it was her excellent presentation on *Trovatore* for my film and opera seminar that inspired me to look for the Marx Brothers' contesting of its popularity. When I realized, during the months of listening in which I was deciding on the examples for the third chapter, that I wanted to ground my case about opera, in the context of the two preceding chapters, on *Pelléas*, I expected a fair amount of grief on that account alone, fearing that it would seem archaic or precious in the light of my insistent obviousness, or insistence on obviousness, in the other examples. The following year there turned out to be at least four new significant productions of the piece in Europe, associated with names no less formidable than those of Pierre Boulez, Peter Brook, and Peter Sellars. Perhaps I enjoy too much imagining that there are good reasons for such coincidences. Wayne Koestenbaum's remarkable *The Queen's Throat: Opera, Homosexuality, and the Mystery of Desire* was recommended to me not long after I returned to Cambridge from delivering the Jerusalem lectures. Like Clément's *Opera, or the Undoing of Women*, Koestenbaum's book may be distanced as about opera on the ground that it does not discuss the details of the music of operas (and in his case, mostly not the words either, or the plots). But both books are, marvelously, about the cultural plot of opera, about the astounding fact of its existence and the facts of the work it does, low and high. You can say that they are about the experience of opera; but then say that analyses of music and of libretti that are foreign to the experience they convey are not analyses of opera. While I regard these books as interestingly tense in the presence of each other, Koestenbaum's single mention of Clément's work takes it as, in advance, refusing his: "One critic who objects to the gay cult of Callas is Catherine Clément, who writes, in *Opera, or the Undoing of Women*: 'Come on, men, shut up. You are living off her. Leave this woman alone, whose job it was to wear gracefully your repressed homosexual fantasies.'" I am sure that when I went past this passage in reading Clément I imagined its addressee differently than Koestenbaum does, not as an objection to the gay cult, whose homosexual fantasies are not exactly repressed, and of whose existence I, surely not I alone, was until Koestenbaum's book at best dimly aware; but rather as an objection leveled at the men in her life ("Next to me is the man I love"), so rather, put otherwise, addressed to the likes of me. All this is for the future, perhaps, but at the moment I am too sensible of the value of both these temperaments in thinking, for example, about the diva's body—about the utter contingency together with the ineluctable necessity in its being just this body that projects just that voice as beside itself, by itself—to imagine giving either of them up.

From the beginning of my philosophical writing, and increasingly in recent years, I have intermittently allowed the draw of autobiography to announce itself, and this tendency has elicited questions, sometimes friendly. Sometimes the questions have been couched in terms of the "personal" manner of my writing, a hasty, and to my way of thinking, misguided description. Various allusions I have in the past made, in particular, to facts of my Jewish background were brought objectively but forcibly to my attention in conversations with Rael Meyerowitz, who, on moving to Harvard and New England from Hebrew University, where we had met, began noticing such recurrences in other Jewish-American academics as well, also characteristically bearing on their encounters with the Emerson tradition of American thought. He is now in the process of completing a fascinating book-length study of the phenomenon.

The rather more systematic, or concentrated, sequence of autobiographical exercises in my first chapter received, after its presentation in Jerusalem, the attentive discussion I had hoped for, given the sequence of motives that had led me to open my lectures with them—that I had to begin these stories, that I had to show their beginning in philosophizing, that I could not begin them without the difficult matter of the story of the name, that Jerusalem permitted my learning to tell about them publicly. Of the many voices I have taken away from those discussions I cite two as emblematic: Isaac Nevo's intervention concerning the meaning of the exhaustion of words, or perhaps confusion of tongues, between parents and children; and Leona Toker's provision of possible transcriptions of my family's Polish name, together with an interested, clear if somewhat implied, question to me about how far I felt what I called my father's lack of any ordinary language spoke to a consequence, in Israel, of what is known as the miracle of the preservation of Hebrew—the fact that so many gifted, articulate, and admiring speakers of it have come to it late, that is to say, as immigrants. However far that will change, it is a part of the history of the miracle.

Before ending by identifying the dedicatees of each of these essays, I express my gratitude to Hebrew University and Harvard University Press for the honor of the invitation to prepare the lectures; to Rector (now President) Hanoch Gutfreund, Professor Sanford Budick, and Dean Menachem Milson, for their respective, thoughtful introductions on the occasion of the lectures; to Dorothy Harman, who among other things represents Harvard Press in Israel, for her astounding resourcefulness in making a brief, complicated stay so agreeable and creative for me and for my wife, Cathleen, for our sons, Benjamin and David, and for Cathleen's sister Stephanie, who accompanied us; and to our friends in Jerusalem, with whom the threads of conversation mercifully, over the distances of space and time, continue their design.

At Harvard University Press in Cambridge, Lindsay Waters, among other courtesies, elicited readers' reports whose thoughtfulness helped in the rewriting; and Nancy Clemente's patience and scrupulousness of eye and ear in editing are a permanent cause of gratitude. I would not have been able to submit the manuscript for its scheduled season without the assistance of Alice Crary, a graduate student of philosophy at Pittsburgh who happened to be spending the year at Harvard, whose marvelous intelligence, tact, and good will carried forward all the various labors in concluding the process of revision that had fallen still when the ever-resourceful author of the manuscript contrived to break his writing arm. She, in addition, prepared the Bibliography and the Indexes.

The third chapter, on opera, is dedicated to the memory of my friend Judith Shklar, conversations with whom could be about anything and everything, but the last with me, just weeks before her sudden death the summer I was writing these lectures, was about opera. The second chapter is dedicated to my grandson Alexander, five years into the beginning of what I hope will continue to be a blessed journey. The first chapter is dedicated to the memory of Yochanan Budick, a friend to me, to Cathleen, to Benjamin, and to David, each differently. His life in Jerusalem and his death there are bound up for me with the all but unbearable significance of the place. I end by quoting, in translation, the first paragraph of a story carried by the Jerusalem papers on the day of Yochanan's funeral. In identifying him as the subject of the story I am revealing nothing unknown to the hundreds of people who attended the funeral. "The lives of two Jerusalemites and a woman from Ramallah were saved yesterday thanks to organ donations by a fifteen-year-old boy, who died the day before at Hadassah Ein Kerem Hospital after a serious head injury." On one real, ordinary day in Jerusalem, whatever else was happening, the end of the days of a young man of that city, a Jew, provided continuation to the days of, among others, an Arab woman from Ramallah. It rebukes hopelessness.

∿ Subject Index

∾ Name Index

9 780674 669819